Sure Can Use a Little

GOOD NEWS

12 Gospel Plays in Rhyme

Jeffrey E. Burkart

CPH®

SAINT LOUIS

To Martha, John, Kelly, David, and Andrew

All Scripture quotations are taken from the HOLY BIBLE, NEW INTERNATIONAL VERSION®. NIV®. Copyright © 1973, 1978, 1984 by International Bible Society. Used by permission of Zondervan Publishing House. All rights reserved.

Copyright © 1996 Concordia Publishing House
3558 S. Jefferson Avenue, St. Louis, MO 63118-3968
Manufactured in the United States of America

Library of Congress Cataloging-in-Publication Data

Burkart, Jeffrey E., 1948–
    Sure can use a little good news : 12 Gospel plays in rhyme / Jeffrey E. Burkart.
      p. cm.
    ISBN 0-570-04866-4
    1. Drama in public worship. 2. Drama in Christian education. 3. Christian drama, American. 4. Verse drama, English. 5. Jesus Christ—Drama. I. Title
BV289.B87 1996
246′ .7—dc20

           96-5315

1   2   3   4   5   6   7   8   9   10   05   04   03   02   01   00   99   98   97   96

Contents

Introduction

Be it known that within the pages of this book are to be found:

Twelve Bible stories told in rhyme;
You'll find them poignant and sublime.
Each of these stories is poetic
And, what's more, each is prophetic!
They are all meant to be performed
Dramatically, so be forewarned,
That as you speak in voices bold,
The Gospel's message will unfold.

This book contains a set of 12 Gospel plays in rhyme based on parables and events from Jesus' ministry. They are designed to be performed by young people in middle school and high school as well as by adults. Younger children can perform some of the shorter plays.

The plays may be used in a variety of church and educational settings—as chancel dramas; choral readings of the Gospel lesson; Sunday school or vacation Bible school openings or closings; puppet plays; school chapel services; or youth or adult Bible study discussion starters. The plays can be presented as thoroughly rehearsed performances or can be done as readers theater with a minimum of rehearsal. You may wish to follow the play with a prayer, devotion, discussion, or Bible study based on the Good News presented.

A performance can take place on a stage, in the chancel area of your church, in a classroom, or in-the-round in your gymnasium or fellowship hall. Note that each line of dialog is numbered for easy reference in rehearsal. Narration can be shared by several actors, or parts can be doubled up, to suit the number of players available. Props and costumes may be as simple or as elaborate as you desire.

To begin a play, have the characters enter the acting area and take their places in the positions from which the action will begin. Once they are in place, they should "freeze" in their positions and wait for the narrator to enter and begin the play. They remain frozen in position until the narrator speaks the first line.

Remember that these plays can be performed in a number of ways—readers theater, puppet theater, conventional play format, or poetry reading. Use your creativity to perform them in ways that will work best in your particular setting.

May God richly bless your proclamation of the Good News through these Gospel rhyme plays.

Jeffrey E. Burkart

No Vacancies

For David and Katherine Mennicke

The Play Begins

Narrators and CAESAR come forward and speak directly to the audience. Crowd enters and surrounds CAESAR as he speaks.

Narrator 1:

1. Augustus Caesar was a man with whom one didn't mess.
2. He was the emperor of Rome and wanted to assess
3. How many people lived within his Roman universe.
4. And so he sent out this decree, for better or for worse,
5. To ev'ry person who was living in his Roman lands.
6. He said,

Caesar *(with the confidence of a TV salesperson and with gestures to milk the lines):*

7. Come on and listen up! I've got a few commands.
8. I need to take a census. I must count heads, if you please,
9. Because I need to tax you all and give a little squeeze
10. To ev'ry purse and wallet and to ev'ry bank account.
11. You need to render cash to me, whatever the amount,
12. For I must pay for public works that make your life so sweet
13. Like aqueducts and Roman roads on which you place your feet.
14. And don't forget I need to know how many I can draft
15. So that my Roman legions can be adequately staffed.
16. This *Pax Romana* isn't cheap, so here's what you must do—
17. To stand up and be counted, you must keep a rendezvous.
18. Go to the place that you hold dear, to your ancestral home,
19. Where you will find a friendly representative of Rome.
20. And there you simply register so we can be precise,

Characters

Narrators 1–3 *(More narrators can be used if necessary.)*

Caesar

Mary

Joseph

Gabriel

Elizabeth

Angels 1 and 2

Hotel Manager

Shepherds 1 and 2

Extras: Angel Chorus, Shepherds, Travelers, Roman Citizens, Townsfolk. *(Thirty or more can be in the cast if desired.)*

Performance Notes

Props are not necessary for this play. Angels may be dressed in white robes. A spotlight can be focused on Caesar, angels, Mary, Elizabeth, the shepherds, and other characters as needed. A crowd can surround the narrators and Caesar as they begin. Lines are spoken quickly and with rhythm. *Approximate performance time: 13–16 minutes.*

21. As from the bread you've earned this year, we take our little slice.

22. Remember that you must comply with all things Romanorum;

23. Just send your check direct to me, care of the Roman forum.

(CAESAR exits.)

Narrator 2:

24. To this decree each person in the empire did comply.

25. And this great census happened when there lived a famous guy

26. Who had the name Quirinius, who governed all of Syria,

27. Far in the eastern part of Rome, southwest of cold Siberia.

(Travelers walk to their "towns.")

28. And ev'ryone went back to towns wherein they had been born.

29. They traveled from both far and near, from evening until morn,

30. Until they made it to the place where they could be enrolled—

31. And small town populations grew at least a hundredfold.

(JOSEPH and MARY come forward and walk in place as NARRATOR 3 continues.)

Narrator 3:

32. Amid these trav'lers was a man named Joseph who had come

33. From Nazareth in Galilee. His feet were sore and numb

34. 'Cause he had walked for 90 miles with nary a delay,

35. For to Judea's Bethlehem, he had to make his way.

Narrator 1:

36. Because he was of David's line, he had to make the trip.

37. Off David's block this man named Joe was certainly a chip.

38. So back to old King David's town poor Joseph had to roam,

39. Because the town of Bethlehem was his ancestral home.

(JOSEPH points to MARY.)

40. But there was someone else with whom he traveled on his way.

41. She too was born of David's line and, I am glad to say,

42. That she'd been handpicked by the Lord to bear His own dear Son.

43. Her name was Mary and her Child would someday be the one

44. Who'd be the Savior of the world and set all people free

45. From sinfulness and Satan's power to live eternally.

(JOSEPH and MARY face each other. As NARRATOR 1 continues, MARY pantomimes telling JOSEPH about the angel's visit. He slaps his hand on his forehead in surprise.)

46. Please understand that Joe and Mary were about to tie

47. The wedding knot. But they were chaste, and Joseph thought he'd die

48. When he was told about how Mary was now great with child,

49. For Joseph was a righteous man who knew she'd be reviled

50. By people who would think the worse of Mary—what disgrace!

51. So Joseph thought,

Joseph *(to audience):*

52. A quick divorce will help her to save face.

(MARY stands apart. JOSEPH goes to sleep.)

Narrator 2:

53. You see, engagement in those days was binding as a marriage.

54. All bets were off if up the aisle you wheeled a baby carriage.

55. The law was clear—she would be stoned if she had been untrue.

56. And so a quiet, quick divorce was all that Joe could do.

57. But in a dream an angel came to help him in his strife.

58. The angel said,

(JOSEPH turns in his sleep as ANGEL 1 speaks.)

Angel 1:

59. Don't be afraid to take her as your wife.

60. For by His Holy Spirit God has caused this Child to be.

61. And He will save His people now for all eternity.

Narrator 2:

62. When Joseph woke, he did just what the angel told him to.

(JOSEPH goes to MARY, hugs her, and brings her home.)

63. And Mary was brought to his home without much more ado.

Narrator 3 *(to audience):*

64. But let's back further up to the beginning of this tale

(JOSEPH and MARY go into "reverse," as if running a film backward. JOSEPH exits; MARY sits on the stage after a few backward steps. GABRIEL enters.)

65. When God sent angel Gabriel to say a word of,

Gabriel:

66. Hail!

Narrator 3:

67. To Mary, a young virgin girl, who got a big surprise

68. As Gabriel the angel stood before her very eyes

69. And said,

Gabriel:

70. I bring you greetings from the Lord up in the sky.

71. God said that I should tell you that you're favored from on high!

72. The Lord is with you, Mary, and I'm proud as I can be

73. To tell you that you are the one spoke of in prophecy.

74. You are to be the bearer of God's one and only Son.

75. I know these words might frighten you, but wait, I'm not yet done!

76. Don't be afraid, for you have found great favor in God's sight.

77. You will give birth to God's own Son, and things will turn out right.

78. This Child shall be called Jesus, and His kingdom will not end.

79. For He's the promised Savior, and on Him you can depend.

Mary *(agitated):*

80. How can this be!

Narrator 3:

81. She cried aloud.

Mary:

82. How can I have a son?

83. I am a virgin; this can't be. I cannot be the one!

Narrator 1:

84. The angel Gabriel replied,

Gabriel:

85. The Holy Spirit's power

86. Is soon to overshadow you, and so, within the hour,

87. A miracle will happen that is from the Lord Most High.

88. With God all things are possible, on that you can rely!

89. And what is more, I've got good news about someone you know.

90. Your relative Elizabeth is soon to undergo

91. A birthing process of her own, and just in three month's time,

92. She'll have a baby of her own, now isn't that sublime!

93. I know that everybody thinks she's too old to conceive,

94. But it's the truth, she'll have a son, on that you can believe.

95. For nothing is impossible with God,

Narrator 1:

96. Said Gabriel.

Gabriel:

97. With God all things are possible, and all things turn out well!

Narrator 1:

98. Then Mary said,

Mary *(humbly):*

99. I am the servant of the Lord today.

100. And now may all these things be unto me just as you say.

(GABRIEL exits.)

Narrator 2:

101. The angel left her standing there, filled with expectant joy,

102. For Mary knew that Jesus was to be her baby boy.

(MARY pantomimes packing a bag.)

103. The next day Mary packed her bags and took a small vacation

(ELIZABETH enters.)

104. To see her old friend 'Lizabeth and have a conversation

105. About the tidings she had heard about her pregnancy.

106. And when she'd greeted her dear friend, Beth's baby jumped for glee!

Elizabeth:

107. Oh, my!

Narrator 2:

108. Said Liz.

Elizabeth *(with great joy and excitement):*

109. My baby leaps for joy within my womb.

110. And, Mary, I must tell you that my heart has now made room

111. For God's own Holy Spirit who has filled me to the brim.

112. With joy and gladness I've been filled, right now from limb to limb,

113. For you've been blessed far more than any woman on the earth.

114. Your child is also blessed as well, and soon you'll too give birth.

115. But why am I so favored that the mother of my Lord

116. Should pay a visit to my house? I must admit, I'm floored!

117. The minute that I heard your voice, my baby flipped—it's true!

118. And you are blessed for you believe what God alone can do.

Narrator 3:

119. Then Mary said,

Mary:

120. I've got to sing a song with all I've got.

Narrator 3:

121. And then she sang a song that's known as the Magnificat.

122. She sang,

Mary:

123. My soul now magnifies the Lord in heav'n above.

124. My spirit soars, my heart is glad because of God's great love.

Narrator 3 *(to audience):*

125. Please pardon me, I have digressed, but flashbacks help explain

126. Just how we got to where we are. They help to ascertain

127. The background for what is to come. So listen carefully

128. To this narration told by means of couplet poetry.

129. Where were we? I remember now, we're back in David's town

130. Where Joseph and his wife-to-be were looking all aroun'

131. For someplace where they both might get a meal and take a snooze.

132. Alas, there were no vacancies, not one room could they choose

133. 'Cause ev'ry hotel manager said,

Hotel Manager *(One or more hotel managers can say this in unison.):*

134. Sorry, we're all booked!

(MARY and JOSEPH continue to search.)

Narrator 1:

135. They found no place to lay their heads, no matter where they looked,

(HOTEL MANAGER shows MARY and JOSEPH a stable, and they rest. NARRATOR 1 comes to front as lights fade on MARY and JOSEPH.)

136. Until they found a concierge who told them they could stay

137. With animals that take their naps in beds made out of hay.

138. So to a stable they were sent, and then what happened there

139. Would cause Good News to be proclaimed to people everywhere.

140. For in that lowly stable, in a manger filled with straw,

141. Was born the Savior of the world, who would fulfill God's Law.

14

142. He would be nailed upon a cross and bear the sins of all.

143. For us He'd die, this baby boy, for us He'd take the fall.

Narrator 2:

144. But God would raise Him up again, and He would live once more.

145. And to all those who trust in Him, He opens up the door

146. That leads away from death and sin, that leads to life anew.

147. And as you listen to these words, you'll know that they are true

148. Because the Holy Spirit works within us when we hear

149. The Gospel's good news tidings that will take away the fear

150. That haunts us 'cause we cannot save ourselves in any way.

151. And that is why the Christ Child came on that first Christmas day.

(Shepherds enter.)

Narrator 3:

152. And on the night our Lord was born in that poor cattle shed,

153. Some shepherds in a nearby field were shaken foot to head.

154. For as they watched their flocks by night there came from all around,

(Lights focus on shepherds. ANGEL 2 enters.)

155. A light that came from outer space, and soon the shepherds found

156. That standing right in front of them was someone heaven-sent.

157. An angel had appeared to them straight from the firmament.

158. The angel said,

Angel 2:

159. I bring to you glad tidings of great joy!

160. For on this night in Bethlehem was born a baby boy,

161. Who is the one that God above had promised that He'd send.

162. He is the Christ, the Promised One; on that you can depend!

163. Come on, get up! He waits for you! And this shall be a sign:

164. You'll find Him wrapped in swaddling clothes—this Child of God divine.

165. You do not need to be afraid, you aren't in any danger!

166. Get up and go! He waits for you! You'll find Him in a manger.

(ANGEL CHORUS dressed in white enters. The angels can wear helmets and carry swords if desired.)

Narrator 1:

167. Then suddenly from all around the host of heav'n appeared.

168. And every angel in that throng spoke up and loudly cheered:

Angel Chorus *(shouting):*

169. All glory be to God on high and peace to everyone

170. For unto You in David's town was born God's own dear Son!

(ANGEL CHORUS exits.)

Narrator 2:

171. And when this angel army had departed from their sight

172. The shepherds said,

Shepherd 1:

173. Let's go to Bethlehem this very night.

Shepherd 2:

174. And see this thing that's happened, of which angel armies tell.

(Shepherds run to town.)

Narrator 3:

175. And then they went straight to the town to find where Christ might dwell.

176. The shepherds searched the town until they found the Holy One.

(Shepherds see MARY and JOSEPH and bow down and worship Baby Jesus. Shepherds leave and pantomime telling townsfolk what they have seen and heard.)

177. Before the manger they bowed down and worshiped God the Son.

178. And after they had left the Child, they spread the news around.

179. They told what they had seen and heard to everyone they found.

Narrator 1:

180. And ev'ry person that they told was certainly amazed

181. By what the shepherds had to say and how the shepherds praised

182. And glorified the Lord of heaven and the Lord of earth,

183. As they proclaimed the good-news story of our Savior's birth.

Narrators and/or Various Cast Members *(If desired, assign couplets to cast members who do not have speaking parts.):*

184. And thus the Christmas story ends as shepherds now depart,

185. As Mary treasures up these things and keeps them in her heart.

186. But this great story does not really have an end, you see.

187. It reaches back and then goes on throughout eternity.

188. He was in the beginning, and He'll be there at the end,

189. The Alpha-and-Omega Lord is Christ, our dearest friend.

190. For Jesus came into this world of sorrow and of woe

191. That by His death and rising, His salvation all might know.

192. The angel said, "Don't be afraid! The Prince of Peace is here!

193. The Name above all other names has come; you need not fear!

194. Believe in Jesus, God's dear Son, who came on earth to dwell.

195. With God all things are possible and all things turn out well!"

196. And so we praise Emmanuel. "God with us now!" we say.

197. Emmanuel, Emmanuel, He's with us still today!

198. He was in the beginning and forevermore shall be,

199. Our Savior, risen Lord and King, who set all people free.

200. Praise God, from whom all blessings flow, for sending us His Son.

201. Praise Him all creatures here below, for He saved ev'ryone.

202. Praise Him above, oh heav'nly host, now let your voices soar!

(Entire cast raises arms to heaven.)

203. Praise Father, Son, and Holy Ghost forever more and more!

(Curtain.)

Note: If desired, lines 184–203 may be sung to the melody of "While Shepherds Watched" or any other common meter doubled (CMD) hymn. Soloists could sing the first four stanzas with the congregation joining in on the last stanza.

Follow That Star

For Randolph and Judy Sherren

The Play Begins

Cast enters and freezes in positions. MARY and JOSEPH are in one corner of the stage with young Jesus. The WISE MEN and their SERVANT are lying down, gazing at the sky. HEROD stands center stage with his back to the audience. His sages, holding scrolls, stand behind him, also with their backs to the audience. The STAR OF BETHLEHEM stands near the WISE MEN, also with back to the audience, concealing the star. The STAR OF BETHLEHEM always leads the WISE MEN until they reach the house where Jesus is. Then the star remains over the house until the end of the play.

If stage lighting is available, dim lights to black while a spotlight follows NARRATOR into position. As NARRATOR speaks, the STAR OF BETHLEHEM holds up the star. (Stage crew can train flashlights on the star if a spotlight is not available.)

Narrator *(to audience):*

1. It so happened, late one night,
2. A star appeared, and at its sight
3. Some Magi (professors from somewhere in Persia)
4. Looked and overcame inertia.

(WISE MEN excitedly point to star. They mount camels and ride to HEROD.)

5. For these were wise men, not some dopes,
6. And without aid of telescopes,
7. They followed the star 'cross desert places,
8. Making stops at each oasis,
9. Till they came up to a palace
10. Wherein dwelt a king with malice—

(HEROD turns to audience with a haughty expression.)

11. Herod, by name. And his effront'ry
12. Was well-known throughout the country.

(SERVANT holds camels while WISE MEN address HEROD.)

The Visit of the Wise Men

Matthew 2:1–12

Characters

Narrator

Wise Men 1–3

Herod

Herod's Sages

Mary

Joseph

The Wise Men's Servant

The Star of Bethlehem

Performance Notes

Props: Three cardboard (or broomstick) camels. Three fancy gifts wrapped in gold and silver foil. Several large scrolls; one scroll should read "Prophet Micah" in letters that can be seen from the audience when it is unrolled. A large doll (not a baby doll) to represent young Jesus. The actor playing the Star of Bethlehem should dress in black and hold a large cardboard star covered with aluminum foil. *Approximate performance time:* 5–7 minutes.

13. But these Magi, straight from college,

14. Were without this common knowledge

15. When they asked a simple thing

16. Of this nasty, two-faced king.

Wise Man 1 *(to HEROD):*

17. Could you give us some direction?

18. We need a slight course correction.

Wise Man 2:

19. For we're looking for a Child—

Wise Man 3 *(interrupting):*

20. And you'll think this really wild!—

Wise Men *(in unison):*

21. Who is born king of the Jews.

Narrator:

22. To Herod this was not good news.

Wise Men *(in unison):*

23. Herod, tell us, if you can;

24. We've double-parked our caravan!
(HEROD'S SAGES turn around and animatedly look at their scrolls.)

Narrator:

25. Herod then called up his sages,

26. And after they had turned some pages

27. Of manuscripts printed in elite and pica,

28. They found a verse by prophet Micah.

29. It said:

Herod's Sages *(reading to HEROD from the scrolls in unison with a deliberate sing-song style):*

30. If you seek the real rulah, *(Note: pronounced roo-lah)*

31. Go to Bethlehem in Judah.

32. And in that unpretentious place

33. You'll find the Child who'll grant you grace!

(HEROD'S SAGES exit.)

Narrator:

34. Herod put on his face of glee

(HEROD and WISE MEN "stage talk" and pantomime actions described in lines 35–41.)

35. And called the Wise Men privately

36. Into his rec room for a chat,

37. To question them of this and that.

38. He asked what time the star shown out.

39. (He was the king, he had the clout.)

40. So these Wise Men were quick to tell.

41. The king replied,

Herod:

42. That's really swell!

43. Go search in every home and room,

44. And if you find Him, come back soon,

45. So I can worship Him with you.

46. Hooray, hoorah, and hoop-dee-do!

(Entire cast freezes in position.)

Narrator:

47. This of course was all a show,

48. For Herod plotted, don't ya know,

49. To kill this Child whom God had sent,

50. Who would fulfill the covenant

51. That through God's Son we'd be set free

52. To live new life eternally.

(WISE MEN and SERVANT unfreeze and pantomime actions described in lines 53–65. HEROD turns his back to audience and freezes in position.)

53. The Wise Men left, they didn't tarry.

54. Each jumped upon his dromedary

55. And followed the bright star that showed

(STAR OF BETHLEHEM leads WISE MEN and rests above Jesus.)

56. Them to a house, the Child's abode.

57. On the door they did some rapping,

(JOSEPH greets WISE MEN.)

58. Peeked inside, the Child was napping.

(JOSEPH ushers them to mother and Child.)

59. Safe in Mary's arms He lay

60. As Wise Men bowed their heads to pray.

61. Then the Wise Men went quite crazy,

(WISE MEN amuse JOSEPH and MARY with their antics as they gleefully dance around JESUS.)

62. Woke the Child, now up-see-daisy!

63. Tears of joy flowed from their eyes,

64. For in the flesh was God's surprise.

65. "Why," you ask, "these adulations?"

Wise Men *(to audience in unison):*

66. This Child's the Savior of all nations!

Narrator:

67. That is why the Wise Men bowed

(WISE MEN fall to their knees and worship Jesus.)

68. And worshiped, singing praises loud.

(SERVANT brings gifts to WISE MEN who present them to Jesus. JOSEPH takes gifts and shows them to MARY.)

69. Then without thought for expenses,

70. They gave Him gold and frankinsenses.

71. The Wise Men knew that they had found

72. The baby King that God had crowned.

(JOSEPH invites WISE MEN to stay the night. They pretend to sleep soundly.)

73. And so they went to sleep that evening

74. Content and happy, still believing

75. That back to Herod they would travel,

76. And the mystery unravel

77. Of where the Child was now located—

78. This baby boy that Herod hated.

79. Then, upon their pillows nesting,

(WISE MEN stir in their sleep.)

80. They had a dream that spoiled their resting.

(As WISE MEN toss and turn, HEROD turns to audience and nervously rings his hands.)

81. In the nightmare, oh so vivid,

82. They saw old Herod, green and livid,

83. At the thought that this Child's mission

84. Was to give him competition.

(WISE MEN wake quickly and send SERVANT to look for another way home. WISE MEN follow SERVANT around HEROD and his sages, who are looking the other way.)

85. When they rose they sent a scout

86. To find a more circuitous route

87. That would take them home again,

88. Avoiding Herod and his men.

89. Now this story's at its ending.

90. Wise Men to the east are wending

91. Over sands of deserts curious,

(HEROD frowns and clenches fists angrily.)

92. Knowing that King Herod's furious.

(NARRATOR continues after brief pause.)

93. And now the Wise Men know the Way,

94. The Truth, the Life, so they can say,

Wise Men *(boldly in unison to audience)*:

95. Come, follow God's bright shining light.

96. Throw off your fear of death's dark night.

97. Come and believe in God's dear Son

98. Who over death the vict'ry won!

(WISE MEN freeze in position.)

Narrator:

99. So if you're searching for a star

100. To light your way 'cause you feel far

101. Away from God and gripped by fear

102. Because you feel no one is near

103. To pull you out of sin's dark night,

104. Come, hear these words: Christ is the Light!

105. The Light was born in Bethlehem.

106. He lived, He died, He rose again,

107. And reigns on high in heaven above,

108. And shines the light that shows God's love

109. To ev'ry nation, ev'ry race,

110. Throughout all time, across all space.

Wise Men *(unfreeze and speak in unison to audience):*

111. For this new wisdom God be praised.

112. And we shall thank Him all our days

(WISE MEN point toward the Christ Child as MARY and JOSEPH stand and adore Him. Entire cast freezes in position until the end.)

113. For showing us His heav'nly glory,

114. And the saving Good News story!

Narrator *(to audience, after a brief pause):*

115. So go, read, highlight, and review.

116. It's all in Matthew, chapter 2,

117. Of how the Wise Men saw the face

(Spotlights focus on Jesus' face and fade out on rest of stage. Or use flashlights to illuminate STAR OF BETHLEHEM and Jesus.)

118. That grants us peace, life, joy, and grace.

(Curtain.)

He Serves No Wine before His Time

For Carl and Barbara Schoenbeck

Jesus Changes Water into Wine

John 2:1–11

Characters

Narrator

Jesus

Mary

Bride

Groom

The Steward

Extras: Disciples, Servants, Wedding Guests

Performance Notes

Props: Six water jars, 4–5 feet tall, cut from cardboard; several one-gallon ice cream buckets; several plastic glasses; tables and chairs (optional).
Approximate performance time: 6–8 minutes.

The Play Begins

Cast enters and freezes in position until line 7. JESUS and MARY are surrounded by disciples; BRIDE and GROOM stand to one side with wedding guests, servants, and STEWARD. If stage lighting is available, the lights fade to black as the cast takes their positions. Lights come up as NARRATOR enters. Spotlights may also be used if available.

Narrator *(to audience):*

1. Jesus sure did something new
2. That's written in John, chapter 2.
3. He changed some water into wine
4. Without the aid of grape or vine.
5. So pay attention to this story
6. Of how our Lord revealed His glory.

(JESUS, MARY, and disciples pantomime and "stage talk" as they slowly move center stage.)

7. Jesus got an invitation
8. That filled His heart with jubilation.
9. So He sent His R.S.V.P.
10. To the city of Cana in Galilee,

(BRIDE and GROOM come forward, surrounded by guests.)

11. Where the knot was to be tied
12. Between a young man and his bride.
13. Mary knew this girl and boy.

(Entire cast meets and greets one another with gestures and "stage talk.")

14. She was there to share their joy
15. With Jesus and His disciple band,
16. Who came along to lend a hand.

17. From the greatest to the least,
18. They all were there and joined the feast.
19. And with their glasses held aloft,
20. They drank and shouted,

Entire Cast *(shouting):*
21. Mazel tov!

Narrator:
22. Until the feast ran short on wine,
23. And Mary said,

Mary *(to wedding guests):*
24. Oh, that's a crime.
25. I'd better seek my Son's advice.
26. I'm sure He'll fix things in a thrice!

Narrator:
27. Mary went straight to her Son.
(MARY finds JESUS and engages in "stage talk.")
28. She knew that He would get things done.
29. She'd explain the situation,
30. Which had caused the host frustration.
31. For it's embarrassing, you see,
32. When wine's not poured for company.

Mary *(to JESUS):*
33. The wine's run out! What can you do?

Narrator:
34. Then Jesus said a thing or two
35. That needs a bit of explanation
36. And some time for contemplation.
37. He said,

Jesus *(calmly)*:

38. Dear woman, why do you

39. Ask Me for help? What can I do?

40. My time has not yet come, you see.

(MARY looks puzzled as she walks to servants.)

Narrator:

41. Then Mary left quick as can be.

42. But these words of Jesus weren't

43. Said with angry undercurrent.

44. These were words all filled with myst'ry

45. 'Bout how Jesus would change hist'ry

46. Through His death upon the tree

47. And how He'd save both you and me

48. By answering His Father's call.

49. In *His* good time He'd die for all.

50. To the servants Mary went,

(MARY "stage talks" to servants.)

51. Told them that in any event,

52. They should listen to her Son

53. And do what He said must be done.

54. Mary said,

Mary *(to servants)*:

55. Do what He tells you to do.

56. Do what He tells you for He will come through.

57. I don't really know what He's got on His mind,

58. But whatever it is, I am sure you will find

59. That something quite marvelous will be resulting

60. When you take heed of His special consulting.

Narrator:

61. Now nearby there stood six big stone water jars.

62. When filled to the top, they made great reservoirs.

63. And though they weren't full, they were ready to hold

64. From 20- to 30-odd gallons, we're told,

65. Of water that Jewish folks used in their washing

66. To clean dirty hands through a ritual sloshing.

67. Then Jesus said,

Jesus *(to servants):*

68. Fill ev'ry jar to the brim!

69. Fill them with water right up to the rim!

(Servants pantomime filling water jars with ice-cream buckets. One servant dips a plastic glass in a jar and takes it to STEWARD.)

Narrator:

70. The servants did just what He told them to do.

71. They filled up the six jars, and when they were through,

72. The Lord Jesus told them to take the head waiter

73. A sample, for Jesus knew he was the cater

74. Who had a keen palate, and so could divine

75. The vintage of water now turned into wine.

(STEWARD tastes wine and calls GROOM.)

76. This master steward took a taste,

77. Then called the groom with greatest haste

78. And asked,

Steward:

79. From whence did this wine come?

Narrator:

80. (The servants knew, but they played dumb.)

81. He said,

Steward *(to GROOM):*

82. You should serve good wine first,

83. And *after* all have slaked their thirst

84. And gotten drunk on tasty wine,

85. The cheaper stuff will then seem fine.

86. But you have saved the best till last—

87. I must admit, I am aghast!

(Entire cast freezes in position until the end of the play. Lights fade out on cast and focus on NARRATOR.)

Narrator:

  88. This was the first of many signs

  89. That Jesus did in ancient times

  90. To show His glory and His might

  91. To His disciples, who were right

  92. To place their faith in God's own Son,

  93. In Jesus Christ, who is the One

  94. Who came to this world to begin

  95. The work that saves us all from sin.

  96. And if you are burdened by all of your sin,

  97. Hoping that miracles soon will begin

  98. In the life you are living without hope or love,

  99. Remember this story. For God up above

100. Has sent you the miracle you're looking for.

101. He's sent the Lord Jesus who knocks on the door

102. Of the heart that is waiting to hear some good news.

103. He says,

(Entire cast looks at JESUS as He moves center stage and speaks to audience. Entire cast freezes when JESUS finishes speaking.)

Jesus *(with arms outstretched to audience)*:

104. Come to Me! You've got nothing to lose

105. But the sin that is weighing you down by the ton!

106. Come unto Me now and believe in God's Son!

Narrator:

107. Remember that we've been redeemed by God's Son.

108. Through Baptism's waters we're washed and made one

109. With the Father, Lord Jesus, and the Holy Spirit.

110. Shout praise forever! Let everyone cheer it!

111. Proclaim to the world the great wonder God brings

112. Through the birth, death, and rising of our King of kings.

(Curtain.)

Short Changed

For Michael and Lori Charron

The Story of Zacchaeus

Luke 19:1–9

Characters

Narrator

Jesus

Zacchaeus *(preferably the shortest person in the cast)*

The Crowd *(The cast can range from 6–10 people.)*

Performance Notes

Props: A ladder decorated with cardboard limbs and construction-paper leaves to serve as a sycamore tree. Additional props and costumes are optional. *Approximate performance time*: 4–6 minutes.

The Play Begins

Cast enters one by one as NARRATOR tells the story. NARRATOR stands to one side of the stage. If stage lighting is available, dim the lights to black and follow the NARRATOR into position with a spotlight.

Narrator *(to audience)*:

1. In Luke 19, the story goes,

2. Our Lord and Master, Jesus, chose

3. To pass right through an old oasis.

4. And after walking many paces,

5. He found Himself in Jericho

6. And soon upset the status quo

7. 'Cause He sought out, and showed affection,

8. To one whose job was tax collection!

9. So lend your ears to this short story,

10. And learn how Jesus shows His glory

11. To everyone who's up a tree

12. And needs to be from sin set free.

13. In Jericho there dwelt a crook

(ZACCHAEUS enters and pantomimes collecting money from the crowd. With disgust, they count out money into his open hand.)

14. Who got real wealthy 'cause he took

15. Large sums of people's hard-earned money

16. For himself—and that ain't funny!

17. He was a tax collecting chief,

18. Which is to say he was a thief!

19. From every tax collection drop,

20. He'd take his cut right off the top.

(With a big smile, ZACCHAEUS pantomimes counting his money.)

21. Zacchaeus was this fellow's name,

22. And unfair taxing was his game.

23. Zack was well-known in Jericho,

24. But to his house none e'er would go

25. Because his evil occupation

26. Made one cringe with trepidation!

(JESUS enters and walks among the crowd. They surround Him so that ZACCHAEUS can't get a good look at Him.)

27. And so when Jesus came to town,

28. A crowd of folks all stood aroun'

29. And stretched their necks to catch a glimpse,

30. But this caused poor old Zack to wince

31. Because in stature he was short!

32. And so, quite as a last resort,

33. Zacchaeus—who was five-foot-four—

(ZACCHAEUS climbs ladder to see JESUS.)

34. Climbed up into a sycamore

35. So he could view and better see

36. The Man who came from Galilee.

(JESUS walks through the crowd, looks up toward the tree, and calls to ZACCHAEUS.)

Jesus:

37. Zacchaeus!

Narrator:

38. He heard Jesus say.

Jesus:

39. Come down, my boy—come right away!

40. In sycamores you shouldn't perch!

41. Come down, don't leave Me in a lurch!

42. Today, Zacchaeus, I must stay

43. Within your house, so don't delay!

(ZACCHAEUS joyfully greets JESUS and leads Him away from the crowd, which looks on in disgust.)

Narrator:

44. Zacchaeus climbed straight down the tree

45. And welcomed Jesus joyfully!

46. Then to his home he brought the Lord.

47. But people muttered,

Person in the Crowd *(with anger and disgust):*

48. How untoward!

(The crowd nods in agreement, scowls, and looks angry.)

49. Can you believe He's gone to be

50. The guest of one who sinfully

51. Has taxed us all and robbed us blind?

52. This is a cut that's most unkind!

Narrator:

53. But Zacchaeus stood and stated

54. Words that flowed out unabated:

Zacchaeus *(with exuberance and sincerity):*

55. Look, oh Lord! Right here and now

56. I give to You a solemn vow—

57. For half of all that I possess,

58. I'll give to poor folks in distress.

59. And if I've cheated anybody

60. Out of anything through shoddy

61. Taxing of their bank account,

62. I'll pay back four times that amount!

Narrator:

63. Then to Zacchaeus Jesus aimed

64. Some words of *good* news. He proclaimed:

Jesus *(to ZACCHAEUS):*

65. To this house has come salvation!

66. He too is saved—let jubilation

67. Ring aloud 'cause he's a son

68. Of Abraham—a faithful one!

69. For all who sin, the Son of Man

(JESUS speaks both to ZACCHAEUS and crowd.)

70. Came to this place and has a plan

71. To seek and save those who are lost,

72. To seek and save the tempest tossed,

(JESUS extends arms in invitation to audience.)

73. So that they might live free from sin

74. And with My help new lives begin!

(Entire cast freezes in position.)

Narrator:

75. And still today the Son of Man

76. Comes to us with His gracious plan.

77. For Jesus seeks to save all those

78. Who live in sin and who oppose

79. The new life He would have us live—

80. The life of faith where we forgive

81. Each other's sins as we confess

82. That we have sinned, and still transgress,

83. Against each other and the Lord.

84. So come! Receive the grace outpoured,

85. And turn your hearts away from sin

86. And with God's help new life begin

87. In Jesus Christ, God's risen Son—

88. Who seeks us out and will not shun

89. The children whom He came to save.

90. (That's why He faced death and the grave.)

91. So come! In Jesus Christ believe!

92. And His salvation you'll receive!

93. And like Zacchaeus you will say,

(ZACCHAEUS steps forward and speaks to audience with out-stretched arms and uplifted eyes. He holds position for a few seconds and then exits with JESUS. Lights dim.)

Zacchaeus *(joyfully):*

94. Salvation's come to me this day!

(Curtain.)

Roadside Manner

For Kim and Laura LaFontaine

The Play Begins

Cast enters and takes positions. NARRATOR stands to one side of the stage. On the other side, the LEGAL EXPERT is seated on the stage surrounded by the crowd who nod their heads and "stage talk." JESUS stands among them. Other cast members enter one by one as JESUS and NARRATOR tell the parable.

Narrator *(to audience):*

1. A legal expert thought it best
2. To put Lord Jesus to the test.
3. He meant to bring Christ to His knees
4. And fail Him on His LSATs.

Legal Expert *(rising from the crowd):*

5. Teacher,

Narrator:

6. He asked in sweet tones fraternal,

Legal Expert:

7. What must I do to have life eternal?

Narrator:

8. Then this crafty lawyer just sat back and waited
9. For Jesus to bite on the hook that he'd baited.
10. But Jesus, as always, threw back a deep question,
11. (Gave the lawyer a case of bad indigestion).

Jesus:

12. What's writ in the Law?

Narrator:

13. The Master inquired.

The Parable of the Good Samaritan

Luke 10:25–37

Characters

Narrator

Jesus

Legal Expert

Traveler

Robbers *(2 or 3 robbers)*

Priest

Levite

Samaritan

Innkeeper

Donkey *(a person on all fours or a cardboard cut out—optional)*

The Crowd *(optional)*

Performance Notes

Props: Two 4"-diameter cardboard circles covered with aluminum foil to represent coins; a cardboard hotel sign; a money bag; a coat; an empty wine bottle with a cork; a long strip of white cloth for a bandage. *Approximate performance time:* 7–10 minutes.

Jesus:

14. How do you read it, and what is required?

Narrator:

15. The law expert knew, so he got all excited.
16. He puffed out his chest, and he boldly recited:

Legal Expert *(smiling, in a bold, happy voice):*

17. Love the Lord God with your heart, soul, and mind;
18. Love Him with all of the strength you can find.
19. And then love your neighbor as you love yourself,
20. And God will put you on the top of His shelf.

Jesus:

21. You've answered correctly!

Narrator:

22. Lord Jesus returned.

Jesus:

23. If you do this you'll live; you will never get burned.

Legal Expert:

24. Who is my neighbor?

Narrator:

25. Was the lawyer's retort.
26. (He wasn't, you see, such a very good sport.)
27. He knew that he'd given the obvious reply,
28. So he asked this next question to self-justify.
29. To answer this question our Lord told a parable
30. Of a traveling man and of robbery so terrible
31. That if you were found in that trav'ler's position,
32. You'd pray for a house call from Luke the physician.

Jesus: *(TRAVELER enters wearing a coat with a money bag hanging from his waist. Pantomime actions described in the text.)*

38

33. A man,

Narrator:

34. Said Jesus,

Jesus:

35. Was once going down

36. From Jerusalem to old Jericho town,

(Robbers enter and take TRAVELER'S coat and money bag. They beat him and leave him for dead.)

37. When he fell in the hands of violent robbers

38. Who stripped him and beat him with so many clobbers

39. To his chest and his arms and his legs and his head

40. That he fell in the road and was left there half dead.

41. The thieves ran away with their ill-gotten booty,

(PRIEST enters.)

42. When down the same road came a priest, oh so snooty,

43. That he passed right on by that poor man on the ground.

44. He passed right on by him. He just walked around.

45. He thought,

Priest:

46. I can't stop 'cause I have an appointment.

47. Besides, I am fresh out of Band-Aids and ointment.

Jesus:

48. As soon as the priest had gone off down the road,

(LEVITE enters.)

49. Some footsteps were heard of a Levite who strode

50. Right up to the place where the man lay in pain.

51. But he thought to himself,

Levite:

52. What do I have to gain

53. By helping this man, lying there so dejected?

54. Besides, if I touch him, I might get infected.

Jesus:

55. At this point the story looked grim for our friend;

56. With no one to help him, his life would soon end.

57. But then on the pathway, he heard some clip-clopping.

58. He heard donkey hooves and then saw a man stopping

(SAMARITAN *enters and bandages* TRAVELER.)

59. To tend him and comfort him—how he took pity

60. On the poor beaten trav'ler who didn't look pretty.

61. He bandaged his wounds, and he used oil and wine

62. To sooth and to heal, 'twas the best anodyne.

(SAMARITAN *helps* TRAVELER *onto* DONKEY.)

63. Then he lifted him up and placed him on his burro.

64. He guided his donkey around every furrow

65. Until they came up to a nearby hotel

66. Where the man could be tended until he got well.

Narrator:

67. Now the man who took care of the man on the road

68. Was a man of Samaria, so we are told.

69. But foreign he was to the Levites and priests

70. Who'd say, "The Samaritan folk are all beasts!"

71. (In short, if you happened to be from Samaria,

72. People would treat you like you had malaria.)

Jesus:

73. After a night spent with his convalescent,

74. He gave the innkeeper a generous present.

75. He said,

Samaritan:

76. These two silver coins sure should appease ya.

Narrator:

77. (He didn't use credit cards, Master or Visa.)

Samaritan:

78. Look after him,

Narrator:

79. He said,

Samaritan:

80. And when I return,

81. I'll compensate you for your extra concern.

Jesus (to LEGAL EXPERT):

82. Now tell Me,

Narrator:

83. Said Jesus,

Jesus:

84. Which one was a neighbor

85. To the man stripped and beaten by robbers that labor

86. On the highway that leads down to old Jericho?

87. Please, answer Me now 'cause I'd sure like to know.

Narrator:

88. The law expert answered as quick as a wink.

89. He said,

Legal Expert (folding arms and looking smug):

90. It's the one who showed mercy, I think.

Narrator:

91. Then he smugly awaited his pat on the back,

92. But to his amazement Christ cut him no slack.

Jesus:

93. Go and do likewise,

Narrator:

94. Lord Jesus commanded.

Jesus:

95. Go and do likewise,

Narrator:

96. Was all that He handed

97. To that legal expert who just couldn't rest

98. Until he had put our dear Lord to the test.

(Entire cast freezes in position.)

99. And "Go and do likewise" we still hear Christ say.

100. "Go and do likewise" to neighbors each day.

101. So Christians take note of the man from Samaria.

102. Remember that Jesus is ready to carry ya,

103. For like the Samaritan, He paid the price

104. And saved us from death through His great sacrifice.

(Lines 105–118 may be divided among cast members, beginning with the couplet of lines 105–106. Cast members speak to audience.)

105. For Jesus knows all about trav'ling earth's highways;

106. He didn't just watch from His heav'nly skyways.

107. He came to this earth, and He suffered and died,

108. Was whipped and was beaten, and then crucified,

109. Was buried, but rose, and ascended to heaven

110. So all who are hurting would new life be given.

111. So when you feel like that poor man on the road,

112. When you are burdened by life's heavy load,

113. When nobody hears as you plead or you cry,

114. And you are forgotten by those who walk by,

115. Remember that Jesus stands ready to bind

116. Ev'ry wound that you have in your body and mind.

117. He's ready to heal you and help you begin

118. A new life that's free from the curse that is sin.

(Entire cast freezes in position.)

119. Now go read the last half of Luke, chapter 10.

120. Read those great words and then read them again:

121. Love the Lord God with your heart, soul, and mind;

122. Love Him with all of the strength you can find!

123. And as the Lord God is loved by you so dearly,

124. He'll give you the eyes to see each neighbor clearly.

125. For as you walk down the long pathway of life,

126. He'll give you strength to help neighbors in strife.

(Lights fade to black. Entire cast exits. Curtain.)

Lost and Found

For Win and Rita Bruhl

The Play Begins

Cast enters and takes positions. NARRATOR stands to one side of the stage. JESUS is seated on the ground surrounded by crowd who nod their heads and "stage talk." Pharisees stand off to the side. Cast members enter one by one as JESUS and NARRATOR tell the parables.

Narrator *(to audience):*

1. Pharisees and teachers of the law
2. Would gather round and mutter, "Pshaw!"
3. Whenever Jesus ate His dinners
4. With tax collectors and with sinners.
5. Among themselves they'd say,

Pharisees *(in unison):*

6. How crude

Pharisee 1 *(to Pharisees with haughty expression):*

7. To have a knosh with all those rude
8. And worthless people who should stay
9. Among themselves

Pharisee 2:

10. And far away
11. From us, who know just how to act
12. In proper ways.

Pharisees *(shouting in unison):*

13. And that's a fact!

Narrator:

14. But Jesus knew the way they thought,
15. And with a parable they were taught

The Parables of the Lost Sheep, the Lost Coin, and the Prodigal Son

Luke 15:1–32

Characters

Narrator

Pharisees *(3 or 4 people)*

Jesus

Shepherd

Woman

Younger Son

Older Son

Father

Employer

Servant

Extras: 2 or 3 people to double as crowd, pigs, servants, dancers, musicians, etc.

Performance Notes

The parts of the Pharisees, the shepherd, and the woman can be doubled or tripled if cast is small.

Props: A stuffed toy sheep; a shepherd's staff; a large silver coin (cover a 3"- or 4"- diameter cardboard circle with aluminum foil); several pig noses (may be purchased at a novelty, toy, or costume shop; or made by cutting the bottom from a paper cup and covering it with pink construction paper); a bathrobe; shower clogs or slippers; a large costume jewelry ring; farmer costumes (bib overalls, cap, boots, straw hat, etc.) for everyone except Jesus, Narrator, and Pharisees. You may wish to use a recording of square dance music. *Approximate performance time: 15–20 minutes.*

16. A three-part lesson that was keen,
17. Which you can read in Luke 15.

Jesus *(to crowd and audience):*
18. Suppose,

Narrator:
19. Said Jesus,

Jesus: *(SHEPHERD enters and pantomimes actions described in text.)*
20. You're in charge
21. Of one hundred sheep—a flock so large
22. That one of them, without your knowing,
23. Left the flock and kept on going
24. Into the open country where
25. By nightfall it was in despair.
26. Since you're the shepherd you quickly go
27. And search for that sheep, high and low.
28. You climb a mountain, ford a stream,
29. Hike through valleys to redeem
30. That sheep who got itself so lost.
31. You search, no matter what the cost.
32. And when you've found it there alone,
33. With joy you take that lost sheep home!
34. You carry it on shoulders strong;
35. You laugh and sing the whole night long.
36. And when you're home, you quickly call
(Extras gather and pantomime excitement and congratulations.)
37. Your friends and neighbors, one and all.
38. You shout and let these words resound:
(SHEPHERD holds sheep toward audience; entire cast freezes in position and looks toward sheep.)

Shepherd:

39. My sheep was lost but now is found!

Narrator:

40. Then Jesus said,

Jesus:

41. I tell you true,

42. In heav'n you'll hear a great to-do

43. In much the same way. Only more

44. Rejoicings will be heard galore

45. O'er one sinner who's contrite

46. Than the 99 who are all right.

(Entire cast slowly unfreezes and sits on stage.)

Narrator:

47. These words of Jesus should have taught

48. A lesson to all of those who thought

49. That they did not need to repent

50. Because they were all innocent

51. Of breaking any regulations

52. And submitting to temptations.

53. Then Jesus went right on to say:

(WOMAN enters and pantomimes search for lost coin.)

Jesus:

54. A woman had 10 coins one day

55. But somehow lost just one, and so

56. She searched her house both high and low.

57. She didn't take the time to grouse.

58. She lit a lamp and swept the house.

59. She checked inside her husband's socks

60. And rummaged through the kid's toy box.

61. She looked in every nook and cranny,

62. Sought the coin in ways so canny

63. That finally, on her knees she found

(WOMAN kneels and finds coin.)

64. That silver coin upon the ground.

Narrator:

65. And all these efforts weren't outrageous.

66. The coin was worth a whole day's wages!

(WOMAN motions and entire cast gathers around her.)

Jesus:

67. Then, like the shepherd, she did call

68. Her friends and neighbors, one and all.

69. She shouted, letting joy abound,

(WOMAN holds coin to audience. Entire cast looks toward coin and freezes in position.)

Woman:

70. My coin was lost, but now it's found!

Narrator:

71. Then Jesus said,

Jesus:

72. I tell you true,

73. The angels in the heav'nly blue

74. Rejoice with greatest merriment

75. Over one who's penitent.

Narrator:

76. A sheep was lost, but it was found

(SHEPHERD holds up sheep.)

77. A coin was picked up off the ground,

(WOMAN holds up coin.)

78. And great rejoicing could be heard

(Entire cast cheers.)

79. On earth and in heav'n, 'pon my word!

(Entire cast slowly sits and listens to NARRATOR.)

80. To lose a sheep would make you wheeze.

81. And silver coins don't grow on trees.

82. But neither of these two compare

83. To how you'd feel and how you'd fare

84. If you would lose some person dear—

85. Your son, for instance. So draw near

86. And see just how this story ends

87. Before you're on your way, my friends.

88. Lord Jesus said,

Jesus:

89. There was a dad

(FATHER and two sons step forward. FATHER stands between his sons, arms around their shoulders. He smiles broadly.)

90. Who had two sons who made him glad.

91. But much to his surprise one day,

92. The younger one piped up to say,

Younger Son *(turning angrily to FATHER):*

93. Now listen, Pop. I've had my fill.

94. Go to the safe and get your will.

95. I'm tired of living 'neath your roof.

Narrator:

96. (This younger son was so uncouth.)

Younger Son:

97. Just give me my fair share of loot;

98. I'll take the cash and then I'll scoot.

Jesus *(after a brief pause):*

99. Reluctantly this dad decided

(FATHER hands YOUNGER SON a wad of bills.)

100. His estate would be divided

101. Equally between each boy.

102. He split the cash but felt no joy.

103. His heart was heavy for he knew

104. The foolish things his boy might do.

105. It wasn't long before his child

(YOUNGER SON walks away.)

106. Had packed his bags and was beguiled

107. By wanderlust for distant places.

108. He sped from home and left no traces.

109. No sooner had he begun to wander,

110. Than his money he began to squander.

(Cast members meet YOUNGER SON, and he pays out his money. YOUNGER SON pantomimes actions described in text.)

111. He went to night clubs, spent his money;

112. Laughed at jokes that weren't funny.

113. Danced with girls with pretty faces;

114. Went to some forbidden places.

115. He gambled with some shady guys;

116. Was in a fight—got two black eyes.

117. He smoked cigars and shot some pool,

118. And all-in-all, he played the fool.

119. 'Cause very soon he was flat broke

120. For life had played a nasty joke

121. Upon this wasteful smarty-pants

122. Who played around with high finance.

(YOUNGER SON sadly turns out his empty pockets and continues to pantomime actions described in text.)

123. No sooner had he lost his dough,

124. He had to face another blow.

125. For famine quickly spread around,

126. And crops all withered to the ground.

127. He had to tighten up his belt.

128. He said,

Younger Son:

129. I'm getting pretty svelte

130. From lack of food. I am in need
131. Of something on which I can feed!
(*EMPLOYER stands or enters.*)

Jesus:
132. So to a citizen he sped
133. With highest hopes that he'd be fed.

Younger Son:
134. Kind sir,

Jesus:
135. He said,

Younger Son:
136. I'm unemployed.

Jesus:
137. The man replied,

Employer:
138. I'm overjoyed!
139. I need that special someone who
140. Can slop my pigs—and you will do!
(*Extras put on pig noses and pretend to feed.*)

Jesus:
141. And so with pods he fed the pigs,
142. But this was not the best of gigs.

Younger Son:
143. I still am hungry,

Jesus:
144. Said the lad.

Younger Son:
145. My stomach's empty, I've been had!

(Pigs nod in agreement.)

Jesus:

146. Still no one gave him food or drink,

147. And so he took some time to think.

Younger Son:

148. Because I was a libertine,

149. These pig pods look like haute cuisine!

150. And furthermore, if I'm not fed,

151. As sure as shootin' I'll be dead!

Jesus:

152. And thus he came back to his senses

(Pigs exit.)

153. And understood all his offenses.

154. He said,

Younger Son:

155. My father's hired men

156. Have food to spare, so I've a yen

157. To go straight home and tell my dad

158. That I know I've been really bad.

159. Tell him, "Father, I'm confessin'

160. That I've learned a bitter lesson.

161. I have sinned against both you

162. And heaven to boot, that's why I'm blue.

163. I am unworthy—don't be calling

164. Me your son 'cause I am crawling

165. On my knees to beg for work—

166. Please hire me on, I've been a jerk!"

Jesus:

167. All these thoughts filled up his mind.

(YOUNGER SON slowly trudges back to FATHER.)

168. He knew that he had been unkind

169. To his good father. So he went

170. Back to the home where he had spent

171. So many happy years before.

172. But as he came up to the door,

(FATHER and YOUNGER SON pantomime actions described in text.)

173. His father spied him and was filled

174. With compassion. He was thrilled

175. By the sight of his lost boy!

176. He ran to him with greatest joy,

177. And in his arms he hugged the lad

178. And kissed his child for he was glad

179. That his young son no more would roam

180. So far away from home sweet home.

181. The son was then filled with contrition,

182. Told his dad of his condition,

183. Said,

Younger Son:

184. Oh, Father, I've been rotten—

(YOUNGER SON kneels at FATHER'S feet.)

185. Into trouble I have gotten

186. So that now I am confessin'

187. That I've really learned a lesson.

188. I have sinned 'gainst heaven and you;

189. There is no doubt, you know it's true!

190. I am unworthy to be named

191. Your son. Oh, Pop, I'm so ashamed!

Jesus:

192. As quick as you can wink your eye,

193. His father called his servants nigh

(FATHER motions to servants.)

194. And said,

Father:

195. Go fetch my robe of silk

(Servants fetch items and dress YOUNGER SON as fast as they can.)

196. And other clothes of that same ilk.

197. And put a ring upon his finger;

198. Hurry up now, don't you linger.

199. Get some sandals for his feet.

200. And what's more, let's have a treat—

201. For supper, kill the fatted calf!

Jesus:

202. And then they all began to laugh

203. And celebrate for they all knew

204. That there would be a barbecue!

205. Then there was a celebration.

(Entire cast celebrates, pantomiming laughter and merriment. They slap one another on the back and rub their stomachs in anticipation of the feast.)

206. There was feasting and elation.

207. The father said to all around,

Father:

208. My son was lost but now is found!

209. This son of mine was dead you see,

210. But he's alive, as live can be!

(Entire cast pantomimes a square dance with do-si-do-ing. You can play a recording of square dance music in the background.)

211. So everybody shout and prance.

212. Strike up the band, let's have a dance!

Jesus:

213. In the meantime, I should say,

214. The older son was on his way

215. Back from the fields that he'd been planting

(OLDER SON enters and hears celebration.)

216. When he heard sweet sounds enchanting.
217. He thought,

Older Son:

218. Do I hear music flowing
219. And the sound of do-si-do-ing?

Jesus:

220. So he called a servant near

(OLDER SON motions to SERVANT.)

221. And asked him,

Older Son:

222. Say, what's that I hear?

Jesus:

223. The servant, with a smile, replied,

Servant:

224. Your brother's back; we thought he'd died!
225. And so your father, with a laugh,
226. Sent me to kill the fatted calf!
227. Your father said,

Father:

228. My joy's unbound!
229. My son is back both safe and sound!

Jesus:

230. The older brother was outraged—

(OLDER SON shows anger.)

231. Because he thought he'd been upstaged
232. By his squand'rous younger sibling.
233. ('Bout that there could be no quibbling!)
234. He yelled above the party's din,

Older Son:

235. I'm staying out—I won't come in!

Jesus:

236. His father pleaded with his son,

(FATHER goes to OLDER SON.)

Father:

237. Come on inside and have some fun!

Jesus:

238. His oldest son just answered back,

Older Son *(sarcastically, angrily):*

239. Why should I dance and have a snack?
240. Look! All these years I've slaved for you—
241. Done everything you said to do—
242. I never disobeyed your orders,
243. Always stayed within the borders!
244. And yet, dear Father, please take note,
245. Not even one young billy goat
246. Was ever given unto me
247. So I could laugh and have a spree
248. With all my friends! So I'm depressed
249. And wond'ring why I've been oppressed!

Narrator:

250. Now as if that were not enough

(Entire cast freezes in position.)

251. The elder son got really gruff!
252. He continued his oration
253. In the hope his condemnation
254. Would, on his father, take its toll.
255. So listen up—he's on a roll!

Older Son:

256. But this son of yours has squandered

(Entire cast unfreezes as OLDER SON continues angrily.)

257. His inheritance and wandered

258. Far away to other places

259. Where he met some pretty faces

260. On whom he spent all your money,

261. Just because they called him, "Honey."

262. So! Now he's home, and on a whim,

263. You've killed the fatted calf for *him*!

Jesus:

264. Much to this eldest son's surprise,

265. His father looked him in the eyes

266. And spoke with greatest tenderness

267. These words to sooth his son's distress:

Father:

268. My son, please listen carefully,

269. For with me you will always be.

270. And everything that's mine, I swear,

271. Is yours for sure—you are my heir.

272. You see, we had to celebrate.

273. Our gladness simply won't abate

274. Because this brother of yours was dead

275. But is alive again!

Jesus:

276. He said.

Father *(with great joy):*

277. So once again let joy abound.

278. My son was lost but now is found!

(Entire cast freezes in position.)

Narrator:

279. That's all there was to Jesus' story,

280. But it sure was inflammatory

281. To all, who like the older brother,

282. Lacked in love for one another!

283. It showed self-centered Pharisees,

284. Filled with petty jealousies,

285. That they should not be so reclusive

286. And to sinners be abusive.

287. For those who truly are repentant,

288. God's prepared a place transplendent

289. Where rejoicing will redound

290. Whenever one that's lost is found!

291. And when you've sinned and lost your way,

292. And you're repentant when you pray,

293. Remember what you just have heard,

294. And listen to His saving Word:

(JESUS comes center stage. Entire cast slowly turns and listens.)

Jesus:

295. You are worth more, by far, than sheep;

296. And for lost coins I wouldn't weep.

297. But I am seeking to accost

298. The wayward ones who are so lost

299. That they despair of being saved

300. Because they've sinned and misbehaved

301. In ways that keep them from the Way,

302. The Truth, the Life. And so I say,

303. My sons and daughters, come to Me.

304. I lived and died and rose to free

305. You from your sin. So come, confess,

306. And with a new life I will bless

307. Each one who's truly penitent.

308. That's why I came—it's why God sent

309. Me to the earth from heaven above.

310. So come, partake of God's great love!

(JESUS ends speech with arms open in invitation to audience. Lights fade. Curtain.)

Minimum Wage

For Glenn and Marilyn Offermann

The Parable of the Workers in the Vineyard
Matthew 20:1–16

The Play Begins

Cast enters and freezes in positions. NARRATOR stands to one side of the stage. JESUS stands opposite NARRATOR. The VINEYARD OWNER is asleep center stage. Lights fade to black while cast enters and come up as NARRATOR enters.

Narrator *(to audience):*

1. In Matthew's gospel, chapter 20,
2. Our dear Lord Jesus told us plenty
3. About the nature of His love
4. And His kingdom up above.
5. He told a story of some workers
6. Who cried,

(NARRATOR points to workers who stand, shout their line, and sit down on stage.)

Workers *(in unison):*

7. Late coming folk are shirkers!

Narrator:

8. And angrily began to mock
9. The ones who hadn't punched the clock.
10. He said,

Jesus:

11. The kingdom in the sky

(VINEYARD OWNER wakes up and goes to workers.)

12. Is likened to a rich old guy
13. Who owned some land and planted vines
14. From which he made the finest wines.
15. One day he got up out of bed,
16. And to the town he quickly sped

Characters

Narrator

Vineyard Owner

Jesus

Foreman

Workers *(may include 4–12 people)*

Performance Notes

Props: Cover 4″-diameter cardboard circles with aluminum foil to make a large coin for each cast member. *Approximate performance time:* 5–7 minutes.

17. To hire some men to work for pay.

18. He said,

Vineyard Owner:

19. If you will work all day,

(VINEYARD OWNER shows workers silver denarius.)

20. I'll give you a denarius!

Jesus:

21. And so they made an exodus

(Workers pantomime work, slowly becoming more and more tired.)

22. Straight to the vineyard of the man

23. And worked as hard as workers can.

(VINEYARD OWNER returns to hire more workers.)

24. He went back to the marketplace

25. At nine o'clock when, face to face,

26. He met a group of poor men who

27. Just sat around with naught to do!

28. He told them,

Vineyard Owner:

29. Go right to my fields

30. And work my vineyard so it yields

31. A better vintage than before.

32. And when you've finished up the chore,

33. I promise that I'll pay what's right

34. 'Cause I'm a man who isn't tight!

(These workers join others in pantomiming work.)

Jesus:

35. So to his vineyard they did go.

36. They worked and sang,

Workers *(singing in unison like the Seven Dwarfs):*

37. Heigh ho, heigh ho!

Jesus:

38. But back in town there still were some

39. To whom the master hadn't come.

(VINEYARD OWNER returns to hire more workers.)

40. And so the master went again

41. At noon, and three, to hire men.

42. And then at five he did the same.

43. He said to them,

Vineyard Owner:

44. It's just a shame

45. That you should sit here all day long

46. Without a job. Come on, what's wrong?

Jesus:

47. They said,

(Lines 48–50 may be spoken by one worker or can be divided among three workers.)

Worker(s):

48. It's not like we've retired—

49. It's just that we have not been hired!

50. And so we sit here out of work.

Vineyard Owner:

51. Then,

Jesus:

52. The man said,

Vineyard Owner:

53. You won't shirk

54. A kindly offer of employment!

Jesus:

55. And much to everyone's enjoyment,

(These workers join others in pantomiming work.)

56. He commanded them to go

57. And tend his vines with rake and hoe.

58. Then as the sun set in the west,

59. The vineyard owner thought it best

(Vineyard Owner motions to Foreman to come to him.)

60. To have his foreman give a call

61. To vineyard workers one and all.

62. He said,

Vineyard Owner *(to Foreman):*

63. It's getting dark, I gauge,

(Vineyard Owner gives Foreman silver coins to pay workers.)

64. So pay each one a full day's wage,

65. Starting with the last ones hired

66. And going on to those so tired,

67. Who I brought on at break of day.

68. Make sure each one receives his pay.

(As the "first-hired" workers receive coins, they show discontent and anger.)

69. And so the last ones hired received

70. A full day's pay. But it sure grieved

71. The men who'd worked throughout the day.

72. They said,

Workers *(in unison):*

73. Come on now—what you say?

(Workers pantomime and "stage talk" mumbling and grumbling.)

Jesus:

74. Words of anger then were mumbled

75. As against their boss they grumbled.

76. They said,

(If the cast is big enough, divide the couplets beginning with lines 77–78 between the workers.)

Workers:

77. We worked the whole day long,

78. Then these latecomers come along,

79. And for an hour's work receive

80. A full day's wage—can you believe!

81. We've borne the burden of the work,

82. So we think we deserve a perk!

83. How can you give them equal pay

84. When we've worked through the heat of day?

Jesus:

85. The vineyard owner turned to one

86. And answered as to what he'd done.

Vineyard Owner *(to one of the workers):*

87. My friend,

Jesus:

88. The vineyard owner said,

Vineyard Owner:

89. You really haven't been misled.

90. I have not been unfair to you

91. And think it's time that we review

92. The contract that we made today

93. Where we agreed that I would pay

94. The sum of one denarius

95. To you, dear friend, so what's the fuss?

96. I think that you should take your pay

97. And quickly go upon your way.

98. I *want* to give the last man hired

99. The same amount that you acquired.

100. For don't I have the right to use

101. My cash in any way I choose?

102. Or are you envious of mind

103. Because I'm generous and kind?

(Entire cast freezes in position as JESUS speaks to audience.)

Jesus:

104. So,

Narrator:

105. Said Jesus,

(JESUS gestures to the front and back to demonstrate that the last will be first and the first will be last.)

Jesus:

106. The last will be first!

107. The folks in the front will be reversed

108. So that the first ones will be last!

(JESUS freezes in position with arms open wide.)

Narrator:

109. So heed His words and hold them fast,

110. For you will find the tables turned

111. If you think somehow *you* have earned

112. A special spot in heaven above—

113. 'Cause all depends on God's great love.

114. You cannot earn a heavenly place.

115. It's based alone on God's good grace.

116. Your place in line is not assured

117. If you think that by works you've cured

118. Yourself of sin and wickedness.

119. For if you do, I must confess,

120. That like the ones who first were hired,

121. Your pride and envy have bemired

122. You in an even greater sin

123. Than you were in with to begin.

124. And thus Lord Jesus came to save

125. And rescue *all* because He gave

126. His life for *everyone* on earth—

127. He died and rose to give new birth

128. To *all* who fear they won't get in

129. God's kingdom 'cause of all their sin.

130. He came to bring us this good news—

Jesus *(unfreezing and speaking to audience):*

131. Believe,

Narrator:

132. He says.

Jesus:

133. I won't refuse

134. All those who wait and those who crave

135. The resurrection from the grave.

136. What happened yesterday is past;

137. The last are first—the first are last!

138. It matters not what you have done—

139. Repent, believe in God's own Son,

140. And you'll eternal life receive

141. Because in My word you believe.

(JESUS freezes in position.)

Narrator:

142. So never sweat your place in line

143. For you've been given grace divine.

144. And don't concern yourself with pay

145. For Christ arose on Easter day

146. To conquer death and so embrace

147. The world in His amazing grace!

148. So trust in Christ—the First and Last—

149. And in His love, which is so vast
150. That He has taken on our sin
151. So that we might new life begin.
152. For this Good News let praises ring.
153. To Father, Son, and Spirit bring
154. All glory, honor, thanks, and love
155. To God who reigns in heaven above!

(Lights fade. Entire cast exits. Curtain.)

Here's Mud in Your Eye

For Gary and Loma Meyer

The Play Begins

Cast enters and freezes in positions until line 7. BLIND MAN sits with closed eyes and extends one hand, begging. A crowd stands to one side; several Pharisees stand behind BLIND MAN. The BLIND MAN'S PARENTS stand to one side with their backs to the audience. Two cast members hold the blue cloth to represent the Pool of Siloam. NARRATOR enters and begins speaking.

Narrator *(to audience)*:

1. Here's a story that's confusing,
2. But I must admit, amusing.
3. Some parts you will find outrageous,
4. Filled with intrigue so contagious,
5. That you'll want to read each line
6. Of St. John, chapter number 9.

(Entire cast unfreezes. JESUS and disciples move toward BLIND MAN as other characters "stage talk" in the background.)

7. Jesus went from town to town
8. With disciples gathered roun'.
9. And it happened that they strode
10. Past a blind man on the road
11. Who, according to the folks,
12. Was the butt of many jokes.

Disciple 1 *(pointing to BLIND MAN and speaking to JESUS)*:

13. Teacher, why was this man born
14. Without sight and so forlorn?

Disciple 2 *(to JESUS)*:

15. Was it his fault? Did he sin?

The Healing of the Blind Man

John 9

Characters

Narrator

Jesus

Disciples *(3 or 4 will do)*

Blind Man

Pharisees *(3 or 4 people)*

Blind Man's Parents

Crowd *(Cast may range from 7–25 people.)*

Performance Notes

Props: A dark blue sheet or cloth; two 2″- or 3″-diameter circles of brown construction paper; double-faced tape. Costumes are optional.

Two cast members from the crowd will hold the sheet or cloth to represent the Pool of Siloam. Put double-faced tape on one side of each construction paper circle. These circles will represent the mud Jesus put on the eyes of the blind man. *Approximate performance time:* 10–15 minutes.

16. Or do you think it was his kin
17. That brought him to this low estate?

Disciple 3 *(to JESUS):*
18. Were his parents' sins so great
19. That God was angry and inclined
20. To strike his eyes and make him blind?

Narrator:
21. Jesus listened to this query,
22. And although it made Him weary,
23. He gave His interpretation
24. Of this perplexing situation.
25. Jesus said,

Jesus *(to disciples):*
26. Now get this right!

Narrator:
27. (At times these guys were not too bright.)

Jesus:
28. It wasn't any sin parental.
29. There was no aberration mental
(JESUS gestures to BLIND MAN.)
30. That caused this man to be born blind.
31. And just in case you're so inclined
32. To think that somehow he's to blame,
33. I'm here to tell you and proclaim
34. That God's great works are on display
35. In this man's life, so don't dismay.

Narrator:
36. He said,

Jesus:

37. The night is coming fast;

38. The daylight hours just will not last.

39. No one can work in dark of night,

40. And so God sent Me—I'm the Light

41. That lights the world and shows God's grace

42. To all the blind in every place.

Narrator:

43. Then Jesus spat upon the ground

(JESUS pantomimes spitting and making mud pies. He picks up the two construction paper circles and sticks them over BLIND MAN's eyes.)

44. And made mud pies which soon were found

45. Upon the eyes of that blind man.

46. Imagine that now, if you can!

Jesus *(to BLIND MAN):*

47. Now, go!

Narrator:

48. He said.

Jesus:

49. Wash in the foam;

50. Wash in the pool that's called Siloam.

(JESUS moves BLIND MAN in direction of Pool of Siloam.)

Narrator:

51. And that is where the blind man went—

(BLIND MAN staggers to Pool of Siloam. Cast members holding sheet make waves as he washes mud patches off of eyes.)

52. Siloam, after all, means "sent."

53. Sent by Jesus to that pool,

54. He bathed in waters clear and cool.

55. When he'd washed the mud away,

(BLIND MAN goes to his parents. They pantomime amazement.)

56. He went straight home, he knew the way.

57. He jumped for joy and sang with glee;

(BLIND MAN covers his eyes with his hands and then reveals his eyes as described in line 58.)

58. He had been blind but now could see.

(NARRATOR gestures to crowd.)

59. Some neighbors thought they had him pegged.

(Crowd nods their heads and pantomimes recognition of BLIND MAN.)

60. He was the blind man who had begged

61. For alms beside the road each day.

Crowd *(in unison):*

62. It's him for sure, hip-hip hurray!

Narrator:

63. But others then began to frown.

64. They said,

Some People in Crowd *(mockingly):*

65. Go on, get outta town!

(Crowd makes mocking gestures.)

66. This man was never blind you see,

67. On this point we should all agree!

Narrator:

68. Then the man rose up and spoke.

69. He said,

Blind Man *(to crowd):*

70. Hey listen, it's no joke!

71. I'm not saying this to tease ya;

72. Some of you must have amnesia.

73. I'm the man who had no sight.

74. I used to beg with all my might.

75. It's me, I tell you—it's for sure.

76. I once was blind but got the cure.

Narrator:

77. They asked,

Crowd *(in unison):*

78. How did your eyes get open?

Narrator:

79. He replied,

Blind Man:

80. I sure was hopin'

81. That you'd ask me how I am peeking,

82. And with open eyes am seeking

83. Jesus, the Man who put some pies

84. Of spit and soil upon my eyes.

85. This same Man ordered me to roam

86. Into the waters of Siloam,

(BLIND MAN points to cast members who make waves with sheet.)

87. Where I went and scrubbed away

88. At these old eyes concealed in clay.

89. And it is simple as can be—

90. I washed, and now my eyes can see.

(Cast members put sheet down and join crowd.)

Crowd *(in unison):*

91. Where is He?

Narrator:

92. They asked.

Crowd *(in unison):*

93. Come and show!

Narrator:

94. The man replied,

Blind Man (*shaking head from side to side*):

95. I just don't know.

(*Entire cast freezes in position.*)

Narrator:

96. Now here is something I should say,
97. The man was healed on Sabbath day.
98. And since no one was an optician,
99. There had to be an inquisition.

(*Entire cast takes* BLIND MAN *to Pharisees. Pharisees pantomime skepticism as described in text.*)

100. And so as quick as you could please,
101. They took him to the Pharisees,
102. Who questioned him. Each was a skeptic.
103. They checked his eyes for antiseptic.
104. Then they asked,

Pharisees (*in unison*):

105. How can it be
106. That both your blind eyes now can see?

(BLIND MAN *pantomimes washing eyes as Pharisees pull out their hair in disbelief.*)

Narrator:

107. After he had told his saga,
108. All the Pharisees want gaga.
109. When they thought about this tale,
110. Each and every one went pale.
111. They said,

Pharisees (*in unison*):

112. This Man is not from God,
113. This Jesus who spits on the sod,

114. Who makes mud 'gainst the Sabbath law—

Narrator:

115. (This kind of thing stuck in their craw.)

Pharisees *(singly or in unison):*

116. He is a sinner, that's for sure.
117. His work on Sabbath is impure.

Narrator:

118. Still others said,

Pharisee 1:

119. These signs spectaculous
120. Really might be quite miraculous.

Pharisee 2:

121. How can a Man who is a sinner
122. Do these things? He is a winner!

Narrator:

123. They argued on. There was a fight
(Pharisees pantomime arguing, then question BLIND MAN.)
124. 'Bout who was wrong and who was right.
125. So that finally, as a last resort,
126. They asked the man for his report
127. Regarding what he had to say
128. Of Jesus and His healing way.
129. The man replied,

Blind Man:

130. He is a prophet.

Narrator:

131. The Pharisees all jeered,

Pharisees *(in unison):*

132. Get off it!

133. Send for his parents!

(A few Pharisees fetch parents to center stage.)

Narrator:

134. Went the cries.

Pharisee 1:

135. They'll tell us whether their son's eyes

136. Were blind or seeing at his birth.

137. We'll hear 'em out, for what it's worth.

Narrator:

138. The parents said,

Parents *(in unison while pointing to* BLIND MAN*):*

139. Yeah, he's the one!

140. He was born blind, and he's our son.

141. But how he sees, we just don't know.

142. Ask him yourself! Now, can we go?

(Entire cast freezes in position as NARRATOR *speaks.)*

Narrator *(gesturing toward parents):*

143. The parents were afraid, you see,

144. To talk too much. For privately,

145. They knew their place; they knew their station.

146. They knew that excommunication

147. Was in store for all who'd choose

148. To speak against prevailing views.

149. If they acknowledged Christ as Lord,

150. By all around they'd be abhorred.

151. And that is why his parents said,

(Entire cast unfreezes.)

Parents:

152. He is of age. Ask him instead.

Narrator:

153. A second time the poor man came.

(Crowd brings BLIND MAN center stage and surrounds him.)

154. They asked him questions much the same

155. About Christ Jesus and of sin.

156. He didn't know where to begin.

Blind Man *(frustrated):*

157. Aren't you listening? I don't know.

158. It seems to me you're really slow

159. To comprehend what has occurred!

160. You fellows are just too absurd.

(Lines 161–162 are spoken deliberately, as if realizing something new.)

161. Or is it that each one of you

162. Wants to become disciples too?

Narrator:

163. Then they shouted insults fistic.

(Pharisees shake fists in fighting gestures.)

164. Oh, they were so pugilistic!

165. First they cursed, and then they muttered,

166. Got so tongue-tied that they stuttered.

167. Talked of how God spoke to Moses,

168. How life is no bed of roses.

169. Yelled,

Pharisees *(in unison):*

170. This unknown fella Jesus

171. Hasn't said a word to please us!

172. We hope He is not here to stay!

173. Where did He come from anyway?

Narrator:

174. The former blind man answered quickly,

175. Made a comment that was prickly.

Blind Man:

176. It's remarkable,

Narrator:

177. Said he.

Blind Man:

178. With your good eyes, you still don't see.

179. Why is it that you so despise

180. This Man who opened up my eyes?

181. To sinners God won't pay attention,

182. Is this beyond your comprehension?

183. God listens to the godly man

184. Who does His will where'er he can!

185. I was born blind, but now I see

186. That Jesus did something to me

187. That never has been seen before,

188. In any land, on any shore.

189. And if this Man were not from God,

190. I sure would think it strange and odd

191. That He'd have power and dominion

192. Over sight. That's my opinion.

Pharisees *(angrily, in unison):*

193. How dare you lecture us!

Narrator:

194. They said.

Pharisees *(in unison):*

195. We've been to school, we are well-read.

78

Pharisee 1:

196. From your birth you've been a sinner.

Pharisee 2:

197. Who invited you to dinner?

Narrator:

198. At this they picked him off his feet

(*Pharisees pick up* BLIND MAN *and carry him away.*)

199. And threw him out into the street.

(*Crowd "stage talks" and gestures to tell* JESUS *what happened.*)

200. When Jesus heard about this trouble,

201. He sought the man out on the double,

202. And asked him nicely as you can,

Jesus:

203. Do you believe in the Son of Man?

Blind Man:

204. Who is He, Sir?

Narrator:

205. He asked real quick.

Blind Man:

206. Who is this Man who cures the sick?

207. In Him most surely I'll believe

208. And unto Him forever cleave!

Narrator:

209. Then Jesus winked at those around

(JESUS *looks to crowd and gives a knowing wink.*)

210. And said,

Jesus:

211. The one you seek is found.

212. He's standing right before your eyes.

213. He's speaking with you so—SURPRISE!

Narrator:

214. He looked at Christ and had no doubt

Blind Man *(shouting):*

215. Lord, I believe!

Narrator:

216. He shouted out.

217. And then he worshiped Christ the King

(BLIND MAN kneels and worships at JESUS' feet.)

218. And thanked his Lord for everything.

(After brief pause, BLIND MAN exits. JESUS moves center stage with crowd.)

219. Later Jesus spoke aloud

220. To all the people in the crowd.

221. He said,

Jesus *(to crowd):*

222. For judgment I have come

223. Into this world so blind and numb.

224. I've come so that the blind will see.

225. I've come to set all people free!

226. If you reject the gift I give,

227. In blindness you'll forever live.

228. So if you think you cannot err,

229. You'll find your vision soon will blur.

Pharisees *(shouting in unison):*

230. What!

Narrator:

231. The Pharisees protested,

Pharisee 1:

232. Jesus, You should be arrested!

Pharisee 2:

233. This kind of talk is most unkind.

Pharisees *(in unison):*

234. Are you saying we are blind?

Narrator:

235. Lord Jesus said,

Jesus:

236. If you were blind,

237. No guilt of sin would any find.

238. But since you claim that you can see,

239. Your guilt remains. That's clear to Me.

(Pharisees scowl at JESUS.)

240. I know it's tough for you to bear it,

241. But if the shoe fits, you must wear it.

(Entire cast freezes in position. Lights fade on cast and focus on NARRATOR.)

Narrator:

242. That is how this story ended,

243. With the Pharisees offended.

244. Each and every one was chokin'

245. On the words that Christ had spoken.

246. But this story isn't through

247. Until I've told Good News to you.

248. Here it is, you sons and daughters.

(NARRATOR points to baptismal font, if available.)

249. Washed in God's baptismal waters,

250. All your sins have been forgiven,

251. And in Christ you now are livin'.

252. But if your eyes still need a rinsing

253. When they tear from sin-filled wincing,

254. When you fear God's not attracted

255. Because you've sinned and have not acted

256. In a way that earns salvation,

257. Here's a word of revelation—

258. The blind man did not earn his sight;

259. It was a gift that showed God's might.

260. For God is seeking constantly

261. To wash us clean and set us free

262. From sin. So hear this invitation

263. From our Lord who grants salvation—

(Spotlight on JESUS and lights fade on NARRATOR.)

Jesus *(to audience):*

264. Hold fast to Me, and ever after,

265. You'll be filled with faith-full laughter.

266. Believe in Me, for I'm God's Son,

267. Who for the world salvation won.

268. And like the blind man, in the end

269. You'll see My face. I'm Christ your Friend.

(Lights fade to black. Curtain.)

Wake-Up Call

For Thomas and Sarah Hanson

The Play Begins

Cast enters and takes places. MARY and MARTHA are on one side of the stage and JESUS is on the other. Narrators may stand center stage.

Narrator 1 *(to audience):*

  1. A man named Lazarus was ill;

  2. No one could cure him with a pill.

(MARY and MARTHA kneel in prayer. They pantomime writing on paper. MESSENGER enters and takes paper, which he delivers to JESUS.)

  3. His sisters, Mary and Martha, prayed

  4. And sent a message to where Jesus stayed.

  5. It said,

(MARY and MARTHA kneel in prayer again, speaking their lines as JESUS reads paper.)

Mary:

  6. Dear Lord, our brother's sick,

Martha:

  7. So please, Lord, come to us real quick.

Narrator 2:

  8. But Jesus didn't need to hurry.

(JESUS pantomimes thanking MESSENGER and sends him away. JESUS sits down and relaxes.)

  9. Jesus didn't jump and scurry.

10. He stayed two days. He didn't run

11. Because His time had not yet come.

Narrator 3:

12. And when, at last, Lord Jesus came,

The Raising of Lazarus

John 11

Characters

Narrators 1–3

Messenger

Jesus

Voice of the Lord *(offstage)*

Mary

Martha

Lazarus

Crowd *(Eleven or more people are needed although parts can be doubled for a smaller cast.)*

Performance Notes

Props: A large refrigerator box to represent the tomb; cardboard cut to look like stones. Lazarus may wear street clothes or a robe with strips of cloth or a sheet loosely wound around him. *Approximate performance time:* 3–4 minutes.

(JESUS goes to MARY and MARTHA. As He walks into "town," the crowd surrounds Him.)

13. The people said,

Crowd *(shouting in unison):*

14. It's just a shame!

Narrator 1:

15. For Lazarus had died, you see,

16. Four days before in Bethany.

(MARY and MARTHA look sad but become happy when they see JESUS. They pantomime telling JESUS what happened as NARRATOR 1 continues.)

17. Mary and Martha were quite sad,

18. But Jesus' presence made them glad.

19. For they believed He was God's Son

20. Who into this poor world had come

21. To save it from both sin and death,

22. To breathe in us life-giving breath,

23. And rescue us from death's dark prison

24. With the words: Christ is arisen!

25. Then Jesus said,

Jesus:

26. I am the Life and Resurrection too,

27. And all who in My words believe will have the life anew!

Narrator 3:

28. Then Martha said,

Martha:

29. Yes, I believe that You are Christ, God's Son,

30. And that You've come into this world to ransom everyone.

Narrator 1:

31. Then Jesus went to Mary, who at His feet did cry,
(MARY falls at JESUS' feet.)

Mary:

32. If only You had been here, Lord, my brother would not have died.

Narrator 2:

33. Then Jesus said,

Jesus:

34. Where is he now?

Mary *(leading JESUS to tomb):*

35. Come this way,

Narrator 3:

36. Mary said.

37. And then the Lord wept bitter tears, for Lazarus was dead.

(JESUS falls on knees and sobs.)

Narrator 1:

38. But Jesus went right to the tomb that with a stone was sealed.

(JESUS goes to tomb.)

39. He said,

Jesus:

40. Now take the stone away.

(People in crowd roll stone away. Everyone waits in anticipation.)

Narrator 2:

41. And then what was revealed

42. Was something that no one had seen in heaven or on earth,

43. For something happened on that day that turned their tears to mirth.

Narrator 3:

44. Lord Jesus bowed His head and prayed,

Jesus *(kneeling in prayer):*

45. Dear Father, thank You so

46. For hearing Me and helping all these people here below

47. To understand that You have sent Me from Your heavenly throne.

Narrator 1:

48. And then what happened could be done by God's great power alone.

49. For Jesus called to …

Jesus *(cupping hands around mouth and shouting towards tomb):*

50. Lazarus!

Narrator 1:

51. … to come out of the grave

52. For only Jesus, God's dear Son, has power that can save.

(LAZARUS appears in tomb's door.)

53. And so the Lord's friend Lazarus walked out of that dark cave.

Narrator 2:

54. And if you find that you are lost and sealed in some dark place,

55. When all your sins have buried you, and you're left with no trace

56. Of hope or peace or friendship or a kindly word of love,

57. Come hear the Good News from the Lord who reigns in heav'n above.

Voice of the Lord *(speaking offstage):*

58. I sent My Son to vanquish death and conquer sin as well,

59. And all who trust upon His name will in My mansion dwell.

60. Believe that He came to the earth and rose up from the grave.

61. Believe that He came to the earth and has the power to save

62. Each man and ev'ry woman, each little girl and boy—

63. That ev'ryone enslaved by sin might sing and shout for joy

64. Because they know the Savior who takes away their sin,

65. And with the Holy Spirit's help can faithful lives begin.

Jesus* *(to audience):*

66. Then like my dear friend Lazarus, you're in for a surprise!

67. And just like my friend Lazarus, you too shall some day rise.

*(If drama is performed by a single reader, substitute the following for lines 66–67:

> *And just like God's friend Lazarus, we're in for a surprise.*

> *And just like God's friend Lazarus, we too shall some day rise.)*

Narrator 3 *(pointing to JESUS as entire cast looks at Him and stretches arms out to Him. Entire cast freezes in position as lights dim.):*

68. For God has sent us Jesus, who has the power to save,

69. And all who on His name believe shall rise up from the grave.

(Curtain.)

Small Change

For Danette and Steve Griffith

The Play Begins

Cast enters and sits around JESUS as lights come up. Some members of the crowd strut proudly on stage, showing off as they drop large offerings in the containers.

Narrator 1 *(to audience):*

1. Jesus in the temple sat,
2. Next to where they passed the hat
3. Where wealthy folk put currency
4. Into the temple's treasury.

Narrator 2:

5. The rich folk came and made a show
6. By putting in a lot of dough.

(WIDOW enters and humbly puts two pennies into the collection.)

7. But then a widow, who was poor,

(Crowd pantomimes laughter—they mock WIDOW. JESUS pays close attention to action.)

8. Came humbly through the temple door
9. And put two small coins made of copper
10. Right into the temple's hopper.

Narrator 3:

11. The coins weren't even worth a cent
12. But nonetheless, the coins were spent
13. Without a thought for earthly praise.
14. And so the Lord His voice did raise. He said,

(Crowd turns to JESUS as He speaks.)

Jesus:

15. I tell you all the truth!

The Story of the Widow's Offering

*Mark 12:41–44;
2 Corinthians 8:12*

Characters

Narrators 1–3

Widow

Jesus

Teachers of the Law *(2 or 3 people)*

Crowd

Performance Notes

Props: You may wish to use horn-like containers for the offering collection and fill money bags or coin purses with coins or other objects that will clink when dropped into the containers. The widow will need two pennies. *Approximate performance time: 2-3 minutes*

16. This widow woman's gift, insooth,

(*JESUS gestures to WIDOW and others as He speaks.*)

17. Is worth far more than all the rest—

18. For this poor widow gave her best.

19. And though she lives in poverty,

20. She gave and showed true charity.

21. She gave far more than wealthy folk.

22. She gave although she was flat broke.

23. And so she's really given more

24. Than those who've given from their store

25. Of wealth—who show off with their giving

26. But know not God's true plan for living.

27. She, in her willingness to give,

28. Has shown us how we too might live.

(*JESUS stands downstage center. Lights fade to black.*)

Narrator 1:

29. But there's more to this simple story—

30. You cannot buy your way to glory.

31. You cannot earn your heavenly place—

32. It all depends upon God's grace.

Narrator 2:

33. No matter how much that you give,

34. Or how uprightly that you live,

35. You cannot pay the price for sin.

36. Your own salvation you can't win.

Narrator 3:

37. But thanks to Jesus, God's dear Son,

38. The price was paid for everyone.

39. And all who on His name believe,

40. The gift of new life shall receive.

(*Curtain.*)

Sonrise!

For Robert and Annette DeWerff

The Play Begins

Roman Guards, Women at the Tomb, and Disciples enter with the Narrators.

Narrator 1 *(loudly to audience):*

1. He is risen!

Entire Cast *(shouting in unison):*

2. He is risen indeed!

(Roman Guards slowly take positions in front of tomb. Women move to opposite side of stage. Disciples sit in back corner of stage, opposite tomb. Entire cast freezes in position.)

Narrator 2 *(moving forward):*

3. Christ has risen and has freed
4. Us all from Satan's deadly hold.

(NARRATOR 2 clenches fists on "bold," points down on "hell," points up on "in that place," etc.)

5. For our Lord Jesus Christ was bold
6. Enough to conquer sin and death and hell.
7. He died and rose that we might dwell
8. With Him forever in that place
9. Prepared above for ev'ry race
10. And nation here on earth below.

Narrator 3 *(moving forward):*

11. And that's why we want all to know
12. About this story of God's love—
13. Of how the God of heaven above
14. Came to this sin-filled, helpless sphere
15. To live among us and to cheer
16. Each one of us with words of grace,

The Story of the Resurrection

Matthew 28:1–8; Mark 16:1–8; Luke 24:1–10; John 20:1–18

Characters

Narrators 1–3

Angel

Mary Magdalene

Jesus

Peter

John

Extras: Women at the Tomb, Roman Guards, Disciples. *(Twelve or more people are needed.)*

Performance Notes

Props: A refrigerator box for the tomb; a large, round piece of cardboard for the stone; a yellow construction paper circle for the seal; a jug; three empty crosses in the background. The angel and Jesus can be dressed in white. You may make a loud noise offstage—bang two boards together, beat a drum—to signal the earthquake.

Approximate performance time: 7–8 minutes.

91

17. To lift us in His strong embrace

18. And call us to renounce our sin,

(NARRATOR 3 speaks urgently to audience.)

19. And through His gift of faith begin

20. To live the life filled with His peace—

(NARRATOR 3 slows the pace.)

21. Because God paid for our release

22. By dying, lonely and forlorn,

23. Then rising on a Sunday morn.

(Lights slowly come up.)

Narrator 1:

24. Early in those morning hours,

25. When darkness seemed to hold its powers

26. O'er the earth as people slept,

27. Some women to a garden crept.

(Women move forward, carrying jugs.)

28. Through the morning mist and gloom,

29. They carried spices to the tomb

30. Of Jesus, who died on a tree

31. Upon the hill of Calvary.

Narrator 2:

32. With spices they'd anoint their friend

33. Who'd come to an untimely end.

34. And so they came filled with emotion

35. In this, their last act of devotion.

(MARY MAGDALENE takes the lead, head hanging in sorrow.)

Narrator 3:

36. Mary Magdalene was there.

37. She hung her head in deep despair

38. Along with Mary, mother of James,

39. And other women who had names

40. That are not known to us today.

41. And as they walk, we hear them say,

(Women walk slowly.)

Mary Magdalene *(to other Women):*

42. Who will roll the stone away?

Narrator 1:

43. Meanwhile, Roman troops stand guard
44. By that stone, so cold and hard,
45. That bars the entrance to the tomb
46. So that no person can exhume
47. The body that was placed inside.
48. For Roman soldiers won't abide
49. Intruders who might try to steal
50. The body placed behind the seal
51. Of Rome that's fixed upon the stone.

(A Guard checks the seal.)

52. It says to all, "Leave this alone!"

Narrator 2:

53. Then, without a word of warning
54. On that mournful Sunday morning,

(Loud noise from offstage. Entire cast loses their balance and stumbles or falls.)

55. The ground began to shake and rumble,
56. Causing all to fall and stumble.
57. Not one of them knew what to do,
58. But all hoped it would soon be through.
59. And then a light came from the skies

(Spotlight or stage light shines from above.)

60. That caused them to avert their eyes.
61. A blinding flash of light as white
62. As lightning on a stormy night.

Narrator 3:

63. The women tried to shade their eyes,

(Women use hands to shade eyes.)

64. When from the light came a surprise.

65. From out of that white shining ray,

66. An angel came and rolled away

67. The stone that sealed the door of death.

68. Each soldier tried to catch his breath

(Roman Guards look around in panic and then faint.)

69. Because they all were filled with dread

70. And fell down as if they were dead.

71. They fainted when they saw the sight

72. Of heaven's angel beaming bright.

(ANGEL enters from behind tomb.)

73. The angel to the women said,

Angel:

74. Don't be afraid; He is not dead!

75. For Jesus, whom you came to see—

76. The crucified of Calvary—

77. Has risen now! Go in and see

78. The place where the Lord Jesus lay.

79. He is not here! He rose today!

(Women rush inside tomb and come out immediately.)

Narrator 1:

80. They rushed inside the empty room,

81. Which formerly had been a tomb,

82. And found that Jesus was not there—

83. He could not be found anywhere.

Angel:

84. Remember,

Narrator 1:

85. The bright angel said,

Angel *(to women):*

86. He promised He'd rise from the dead

87. Upon the third day—that's today!

88. So once again I'm here to say,

89. The Lord is risen from the dead!

90. And what's more He goes ahead

91. Of you up north to Galilee.

92. Tell His disciples they will see

93. Him there, for you can trust His word.

94. Go! Tell them all that has occurred!

Narrator 2:

95. From the tomb the women fled

(Women run toward disciples.)

96. With news that Jesus wasn't dead.

97. They trembled with both joy and fear

(JESUS enters.)

98. When suddenly someone drew near

(Women stop in front of JESUS.)

99. And said,

Jesus:

100. Hello, don't be afraid!

(Women are stunned for a moment, then fall at JESUS' feet.)

Narrator 2:

101. Then at His feet they fell and prayed.

102. They worshiped Christ, their risen King

103. And praised their Lord for everything.

104. Then Jesus said,

Jesus *(joyfully):*

105. Now go and tell

106. My brothers that all things are well.

107. Tell them to go to Galilee;

108. Let each one know that's where I'll be.

(*JESUS exits. Women look at one another, then run to disciples.*)

Narrator 3:

109. Straight back to town the women dashed,

110. And though a door the women crashed

111. To tell what they had seen and heard.

112. But some who listened said, "Absurd!"

(*Most of the disciples shake their heads in disbelief.*)

Disciple 1:

113. We don't believe what you have said

114. About this rising from the dead!

Narrator 1:

115. But Peter didn't stop to think;

(*PETER gets up immediately.*)

116. He got up faster than a wink.

117. And John, who wouldn't be outdone,

(*JOHN runs after PETER.*)

118. Got on his feet to make the run

(*JOHN and PETER race to tomb.*)

119. To see if what was said was true.

120. They ran so fast they almost flew.

Narrator 2:

121. But Peter could not keep the pace.

(*JOHN overtakes PETER and gets to tomb first.*)

122. The best that he could do was chase

123. Fleet-footed John who got there first.

124. Into the empty tomb he burst

125. With Peter who got second place

(*PETER huffs and puffs as he arrives.*)

126. In this great Easter morning race.

Narrator 3:

127. They looked inside the empty grave,

(JOHN and PETER look into the tomb.)

128. But there was no one in the cave.

129. Their Lord was nowhere to be seen.

130. They said,

Peter:

131. What can all these things mean?

Narrator 3:

132. And as they slowly walked away,

(PETER and JOHN depart slowly, pantomiming puzzlement.)

133. They said,

John:

134. What's happened here today?

Narrator 3:

135. But you and I know what occurred.

136. We know about God's saving Word

137. Who was made flesh and came to live

138. Upon this earth so He could give

139. Himself for us that we might be

140. With Him throughout eternity.

(Entire cast assembles behind Narrators.)

Narrators *(in unison):*

141. He is risen!

Entire Cast *(in unison):*

142. He is risen indeed!

(Entire cast listens intently to Narrators.)

Narrator 2:

143. Christ has risen and has freed

144. Us all from Satan's deadly hold,

145. For our Lord Jesus Christ was bold

146. Enough to conquer sin and death and hell.

147. He died and rose that we might dwell

148. With Him forever in that place

149. That's been prepared for ev'ry race

150. And nation here on earth below.

Narrator 3:

151. And that's what He wants all to know.

152. So tell abroad this Easter story;

153. Tell of resurrected glory.

Narrator 1:

154. Tell how Jesus, God's own Son,

155. Has for us all salvation won, and

156. Shout the Easter morning creed:

157. He is risen!

Entire Cast (*shouting in unison with joy and confidence*):

158. He is risen indeed!

(*Curtain.*)

Fish Fry

For Robert and Lynne Holst

The Play Begins

Cast enters and freezes in positions until line 27. JESUS stands in background while disciples come center stage and pretend to sleep. NARRATOR enters and speaks.

Narrator *(to audience):*

1. After rising from the grave,
2. Our Lord and Master Jesus gave
3. Some make-up lessons to His students—
4. 'Twas the better part of prudence
5. 'Cause someday they'd all be preaching,
6. Each and every one be teaching,
7. Of the Gospel's message glorious
8. And of Christ who rose victorious.
9. They'd proclaim the saving Word
10. Like old Nicodemus heard.
11. The words that told of God's great love,
12. The Word that came from heaven above,
13. That through God's one and only Son,
14. The world's salvation would be won.
15. The words of Jesus all should cherish.
16. Whoe'er believes in Him won't perish,
17. And eternal life receive,
18. When on Christ Jesus they believe.
19. And if you don't know what I mean,
20. Go check out St. John 3:16.
21. Here ends the prolog, so take note
22. Of seven disciples in a boat
23. Who took their fishing very serious
24. On the sea that's called Tiberias.

Characters

Narrator

Jesus

Peter

Thomas

Nathaniel

James

John

Two Disciples

Performance Notes

Props: A large refrigerator box for the boat; an empty net, such as a badminton or tennis net; a second net filled with cardboard fish; sticks stacked like a campfire; a loaf of French bread; seven cardboard or Styrofoam fish skewered on a stick. *Approximate performance time:* 7–10 minutes.

25. Now heed the play which is to come

26. From St. John, chapter 21.

(NARRATOR continues after a brief pause. PETER wakes up and stretches.)

27. Simon Peter rose from bed.

Peter:

28. I'm going out to fish,

Narrator:

29. He said.

(Each disciple, in turn, proceeds to boat.)

30. Then Thomas Didymus, the Twin,

31. Wanted to be counted in.

32. So did Nathaniel, from Cana in Galilee,

33. And James and John, the two sons of Zebedee.

34. And two more disciples, just for good measure,

35. Said,

Two Disciples *(in unison):*

36. We'll go with you.

Narrator:

37. And at their leisure

(Disciples pantomime rowing out to sea and cast empty net.)

38. They got in the boat and fished all that night.

39. But I'm sad to report, that by dawn's early light,

(Disciples pull empty net into boat and shake heads in dismay. Entire cast freezes in position.)

40. They hadn't a bite.

Narrator:

41. Actually, they didn't use hooks, lines, and sinkers.

42. They used a big fish net to catch all those stinkers

43. Who, for some reason, just could not be caught.

44. So that night's fishing had come to naught.

(Entire cast unfreezes and continues to fish.)

45. Upon the shore Lord Jesus stood.

46. He knew the fishing wasn't good.

(Disciples squint and shield their eyes with their hands.)

47. And even though they strained their eyes,

48. The disciples didn't realize

49. That it was Jesus who was calling

50. To inquire about their trawling.

Jesus *(calling through cupped hands):*

51. Friends,

Narrator:

52. He shouted,

Jesus:

53. Have you any fish?

Disciples *(in unison):*

54. No!

Narrator:

55. They answered,

Disciples *(in unison):*

56. Don't we wish!

Jesus:

57. To the right side of the boat throw your net.

58. Throw your net over, don't give up just yet.

59. For if you will cast your net as I've instructed,

60. I'm sure that a fish or two will be abducted.

Narrator:

61. These empty-net fishermen had expertise.

(Disciples haul up empty net.)

62. They hauled up the net with the greatest of ease.

63. And without so much as a rip, tear, or tangle,

64. They tossed their net over and started to angle

65. From port to starboard. They let the net slip

66. Into the waters right next to the ship.

(Disciples throw empty net over side of the boat away from audience. Extras or stage crew switches empty net for full net. If play is performed in the round or an open area, keep the net full of fish in the boat.)

67. And as soon as they'd cast the net into the sea,

(Disciples strain to pull up full net.)

68. The net got as heavy as heavy could be.

69. They strained, and they pulled, and they broke out in sweat

70. Because of the number of fish in their net.

71. Then John said to Peter,

John:

72. Hey, look! It's the Lord!

Narrator:

73. Pete dressed when he heard it and jumped overboard.

(PETER pantomimes putting on a shirt or robe and jumps out of the boat. PETER pantomimes swimming or back floating while Disciples pantomime rowing to shore.)

74. He swam through the water. He did the back float,

75. While a hundred yards back the rest paddled the boat.

76. They tugged at their oars as they towed a full net

77. And were happy to get back to land, you can bet!

Narrator:

78. Now Jesus was cooking up His favorite dish—

(JESUS cooks fish over campfire.)

79. Recall what He'd done with five loaves and two fish?

80. He made them a breakfast of fish and of bread

81. Over a fire with its coals glowing red.

82. Jesus said,

Jesus:

83. Bring some of the fish you just caught.

(PETER brings the full net to JESUS.)

Narrator:

84. So Peter obeyed Him and to Jesus brought

85. The net that was heavy as heavy could be,

86. Full of large fish numb'ring 153.

Jesus *(taking a few fish as He speaks):*

87. Now come and have breakfast,

Narrator:

88. The Lord Jesus said.

Jesus *(pointing to fish and bread):*

89. Come and have breakfast of fish and of bread.

(Disciples sit around campfire but are ashamed to look up.)

Narrator:

90. But none of them dared to ask, "Who are You, Sir?"

91. They already knew, so they didn't confer.

(Disciples pantomime eating.)

92. They all ate in silence, some wanted to hide,

(THOMAS and PETER hide their faces when NARRATOR says their names.)

93. Like Thomas who doubted and Peter who lied.

94. And though each man felt the sharp pain of remorse,

95. All of them knew they had steered the right course

96. To the Man who was serving the fish and the bread,

97. To Jesus the true Lord who rose from the dead.

(Disciples look at JESUS, who continues cooking and serving.)

98. Jesus kept serving the fish and the bread;

99. He kept right on serving until all were fed.

100. And this is the work that He wants us to do—

101. To serve one another, from Him take our cue.

102. He wants us to cast out a net to the world—

103. The net of the Gospel. He wants it unfurled

104. To surround every person, each nation and race,

105. In the net of His Gospel's miraculous grace.

(JESUS comes center stage and gestures with open arms to audience. Disciples look to JESUS and entire cast freezes in position until line 111.)

106. And Jesus invites us to eat with Him still,

107. To eat the Lord's Supper and so do His will,

108. To come and partake in His meal so divine

109. In which He Himself comes in bread and in wine.

110. But if you're a sinner,

(One by one, each disciple stands and speaks to audience.)

Thomas:

111. A doubter,

Peter:

112. A liar.

Nathaniel:

113. If you are gripped by some evil desire

114. That keeps you away from what the Lord wishes

James:

115. Remember that you are now one of the fishes

116. That God wants to pull from the deep sea of sin.

John:

117. He wants to catch you so that you can begin

118. A life that reflects the Good News you have heard.

Two Disciples *(in unison):*

119. A new life that's ready to feed on God's Word.

Narrator:

120. So feed on this message:

Disciples *(shouting in unison):*

121. The Lord is arisen!

Peter:

122. He died and He rose! He has broken the prison

Nathaniel:

123. Of sin that would keep us from His banquet table

James:

124. For He is the one who did more than we're able
125. To do for ourselves.

John:

126. For He paid the huge price
127. And ransomed us all through His great sacrifice.

(Disciples freeze in position with arms stretched toward JESUS.)

Narrator:

128. Thus being fed, we are ready to feed.
129. Just as the disciples, we're ready to lead
130. A new life proclaiming His gifts and His glory,
131. A life that shines forth with the life-changing story
132. Of Jesus the Christ who came down from above
133. To give us the gift of His unfailing love.

(Lights fade to black. Entire cast exits. Curtain.)

Record of Original Performance

"Small Change" and "Follow That Star"

Produced at the E. M. Pearson Theatre, Concordia University, St. Paul, Minnesota, on January 26–29, 1995, as part of a larger production entitled, "Gospel Time in Gospel Rhyme." Additional plays and musicals by Jeffrey E. Burkart performed at the "Gospel Time in Gospel Rhyme" production included, "Don't Get Burned!" (a musical based on the story of the image of gold and the three men in the fiery furnace), "The Mustard Seed" (a song and ballet based on the parable of the mustard seed), and "Man Overboard!" (a musical based on the book of Jonah). Six performances were presented to audiences totaling more than 1,900. The "Man Overboard!" musical is available from Concordia Publishing House.

Both plays written and directed by Jeffrey E. Burkart

Assistant Director/Stage Manager Anna Eisenbraun

Cast:

Dan Asmus	Julie Olsin
James Bargmann	John Otte
Melissa Beise	Jolene Pick
Anna Eisenbraun	Jennifer Riggert
Kari Glaeseman	Carrah Rosine
Jamie Guse	Joel Schuessler
Trina Justman	Harvey Slaughter
Laurie Klutman	Rachel Stohlmann
	Ward Yunker

"Lost and Found," "Short Changed," "Here's Mud in Your Eye," "Roadside Manner," and "No Vacancies"

Produced at the E. M. Pearson Theatre, Concordia University, St. Paul, Minnesota, on February 1–4, 1996, as part of a larger production entitled, "Gospel Time in Gospel Rhyme II." Seven performances were given to audiences totaling more than 2,300.

All plays written and directed by Jeffrey E. Burkart

Assistant Director Anna Eisenbraun

Stage Manager Holly Oscarson

Cast:

James Bargmann	Shawn Hecksel
Mark Fuchs	Geoffrey Klass
Anika Gadbury	Jill Marquardt
Sarah Gilbertson	Jennifer Mockros
Rebecca Gilder	Julie Muilenburg
Tami Haupt	Rachel Noennig
Shannon Hecksel	Andrew Posko
	Matthew Wedel